Management
in the
Home

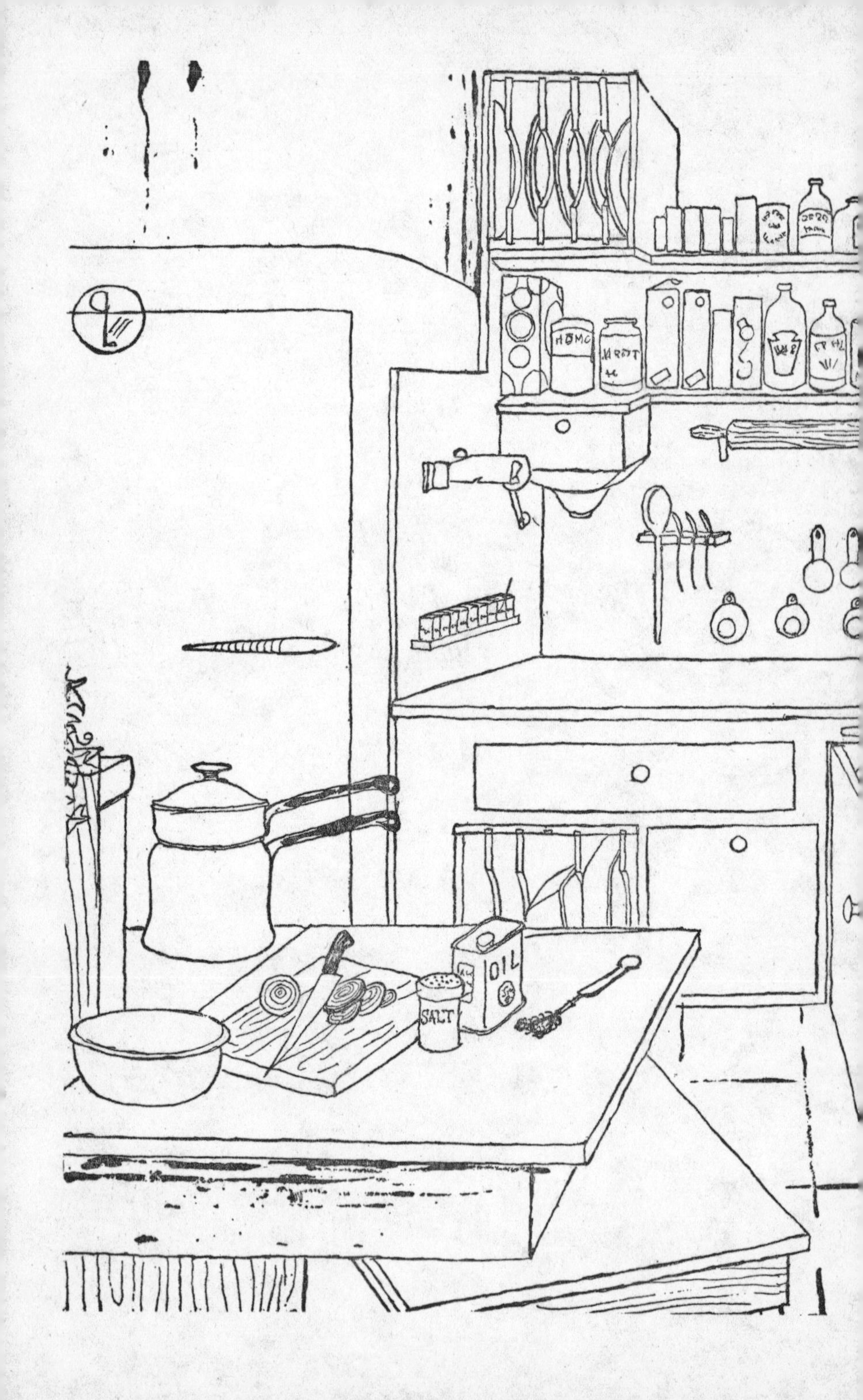
SALT
OIL

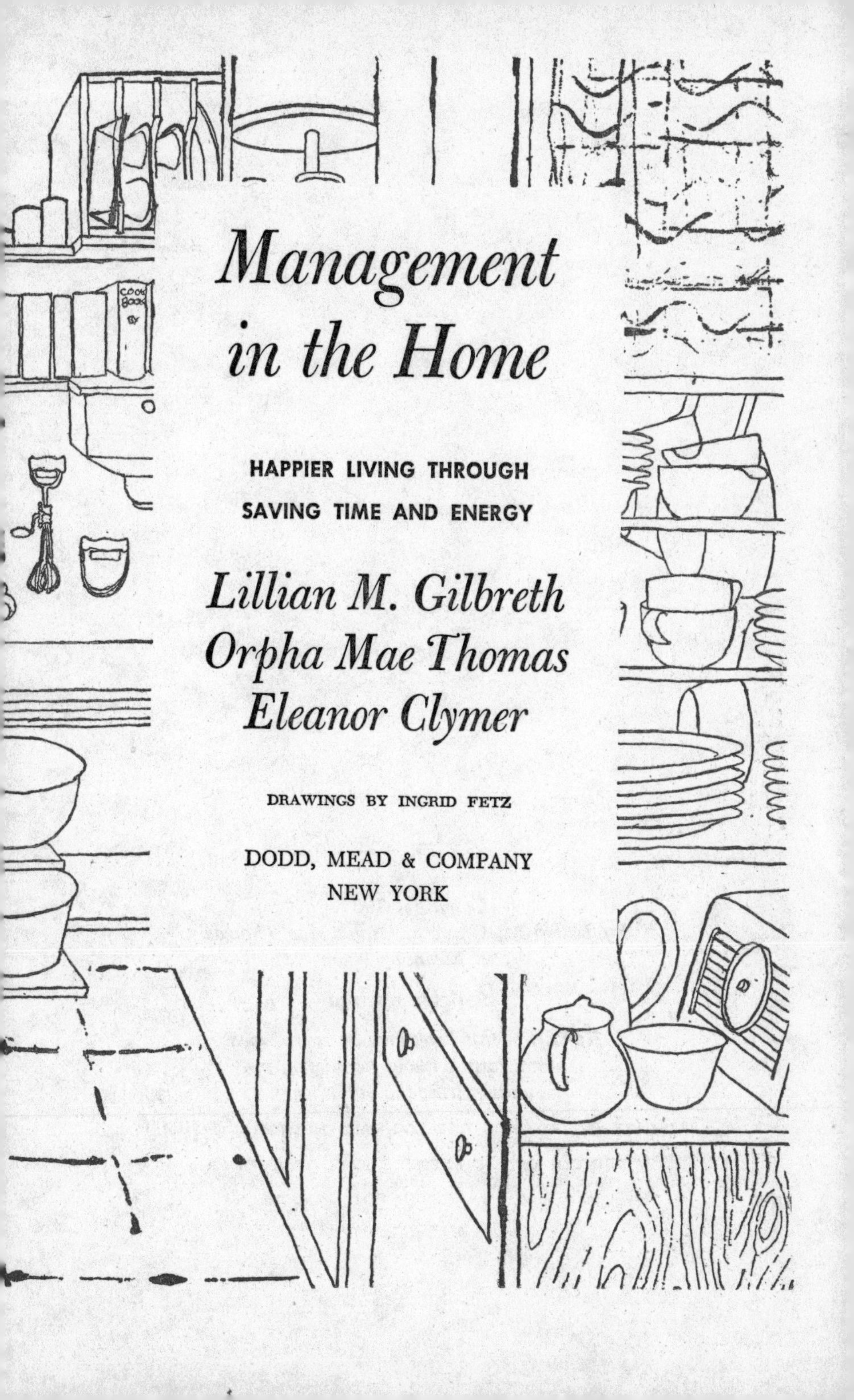

Management in the Home

HAPPIER LIVING THROUGH SAVING TIME AND ENERGY

Lillian M. Gilbreth
Orpha Mae Thomas
Eleanor Clymer

DRAWINGS BY INGRID FETZ

DODD, MEAD & COMPANY
NEW YORK

LIBRARY OF CONGRESS CATALOG CARD NUMBER: 54-10563

PRINTED IN THE UNITED STATES OF AMERICA

Acknowledgments

The authors wish to express their appreciation of the work done in many different fields of research by various organizations, state colleges, and agricultural experiment stations, which has been of inestimable help to them in compiling this book. It is painstaking work of this kind, being done by students and researchers all over the country, which is building up a body of knowledge on the application of scientific management to homemaking, and which has established the prestige of this walk of life on an equal footing with the other professions.

We especially wish to thank the American Heart Association; the Illuminating Engineering Society; the Institute of Physical Medicine and Rehabilitation at Bellevue Hospital, New York; the Small Homes Council of the University of Illinois; the Agricultural Experiment Station at Purdue University, and the New York State College of Home Economics at Cornell University, for the use of their material.

Thanks are due to Miss Jane Callaghan and to the Connecticut College for Women and Teachers College of Columbia University for the use of process charts and simultaneous motion charts.

And special gratitude must be given to Miss Dorothy Bryan of Dodd, Mead & Company for her unceasing patience and help in bringing the work to a successful finish.

Contents

Management
in the
Home

Introduction

SCIENTIFIC MANAGEMENT IN THE HOME

Homemaking is a job.

It takes many different kinds of jobs to keep our world going, and homemaking is one of them. It's a good job and an important job, and it ought to be an enjoyable one. They say it's love that makes the world go round. We willingly work for those we love. If we can also love—or at least like—the work itself, the pleasure is doubled. The woman who likes her job of homemaking, who does it with skill and zest, whose home is well managed and whose family is contented, is a happy woman.

We no longer say, "Woman's place is in the home," because many women have their places outside the home. But the home belongs to the family, and it is still true that the family is woman's chief interest, it is even more a privilege and a trust, whether she has an outside job or not.

What is a home? To the caveman, it was a shelter from enemies and the weather, a place to crawl into when life outside was too cold or hot or wet or dangerous.

To us it is much more. It is there that we are fed and rested, nursed when we are sick, comforted when we're unhappy, applauded when we're successful. To each member of the family who lives there it is something special and personal.

To the husband, it's an incentive and an inspiration. It's the place that houses his nearest and dearest, the place he comes home to after a hard day's work.

To the wife, it is a work place. It's her dream house. It's the hospitable hearth to which she welcomes her guests, the safe haven where she brings up her children.

To both of them, it's a creation, the fruit of their life together.

To the children, it's the center of warmth and security that mother and father have made for them. It's where they learn the important lessons of life—how to eat, walk, talk, play, work; how to love their fellow men, how to hate injustice, and in general act like civilized human beings. From it they go forth to take their places in the world. And when they go, they carry with them all the habits and feelings they learned at home, so that the home comes to mean still more things to more people.

To a businessman, it is a market.

To an employer, it is the place where his staff learned work habits and attitudes. A happy home makes a good worker.

To a politician, it's a source of votes.

To a landlord, it's a living.

It is the home that is the backbone of the church, the school, the museum, the university and the theater, because it is at home that people learn to love religion and culture. And so its influence spreads to the community and the nation. It is indeed true that "the hand that rocks the cradle rules the world."

And yet sometimes the hand gets tired of "rocking the cradle."

The home is a very fine institution, but it has to be kept going by a special sort of labor known as housework, and complaints about this kind of labor have been heard in the land. It seems that it is different from other kinds of labor.

First of all, many of the women who find themselves doing it have not been trained for it, but have had to pick it up by ear, as it were. They went to school to learn languages, literature, chemistry or stenography. But housework, though it is so important, they have been expected to know by instinct. Hence their methods are often old-fashioned and wasteful. Woman's work is never done, we hear. Housework is monotonous. Housework is lonely. Housework is unpaid labor.

Work well done is satisfying and rewarding. But work inefficiently done, without skill and under pressure, gives rise to frustration and unhappiness.

A study was made some time ago in which about five hundred homemakers were asked why they disliked certain tasks such as house-cleaning, ironing, dish-washing, mopping and the like. These are some of the causes they advanced:

Uncertainty as to correct method of doing the work.
Lack of skill to produce quality desired.
Conflicting standards within the family group and inability to satisfy all members.
Lack of approval or appreciation by other members of the family.
Lack of adequate or desired equipment.
Unfavorable conditions under which tasks are performed.
Monotony of tasks.
Conflict between traditional work practices and new developments and methods.
Time required by task preferred for other more interesting activities.
Task requires isolation.
Not enough time and thought given to planning of work.*

Many remedies have been suggested. Women have been advised to take jobs outside the home, to cultivate hobbies, arts, outside interests, to have more social life, to send their young children to nursery school, to use paper plates and prepared food,

* Elaine E. Knowles, *Some Effects of the Height of Ironing Surface on the Worker,* Cornell University Agricultural Experiment Station Bulletin 833, 1946, pp. 8–9.

to take vacations, to take courses. These are all good suggestions. Most of them, however, seem to suggest that the best way for woman to improve her lot is to escape from it.

This is fallacious—first of all because she doesn't really *want* to escape from it, and secondly because it is obvious that *somebody* must and should do the work. A well-managed home is necessary to happy family life. This means work, and work should be enjoyed. Work occupies too much of our life to be hated.

"Find your happiness in your work," said one wise man, "or you will never find it anywhere else."

So it seems better not to abandon the work but to improve our methods of working.

Fortunately we have at hand a very good way of doing this: scientific management.

Scientific management means just what it says: the application of science, including common sense, to management problems. It includes the handling of machines, materials and people, and it recognizes that of these three, people are the most important.

It had its start in industry. For years engineers had been working to make better machines. They had concentrated on improving materials. Then they became interested in labor.

"The human element," they said, "is, after all, what gets the job done. In order to conserve the human element, we must find out what is the one best way to do each job."

By carefully observing how work was done, and by keeping exact records of the time and motion used to do each job, they developed simpler, easier and more satisfying ways of working.

One engineer, for instance, made a study of coal shoveling at the Bethlehem Steel Works. By changing the tools used and the method of work, he was able with 140 men to get the same amount of work done that had formerly required 400 to 600 men. He reduced the cost of handling material from seven or eight to three or four cents a ton. This meant a saving to the company of $39,000 in six months.

Another engineer began his career in the construction business by laying bricks. He saw that no two men laid bricks in the same way. He also saw that an individual worker did not always use the same set of motions. He decided to find the "one best way" of laying bricks. He soon discovered ways of doing the work more quickly and with less fatigue. For instance, he invented a scaffold which could easily be raised to the most convenient working level, so that the worker did not have to reach uncomfortably. There was a shelf for holding the bricks and mortar so that the bricklayer did not need to bend over to pick up a brick from the floor each time he needed one.

These, with other improvements, made it possible for a man to lay 350 bricks per hour, on a job where the record had previously been 120 bricks per hour!

Naturally, in industry, where profits were to be made or lost, these methods took hold quickly. Now every business and industry uses them. Libraries, hospitals, restaurants, farms are getting their work done faster, better and at less expense.

Why should not homes do the same?

The businessman or industrial worker has one job. The housewife has a dozen. She is nurse, cook, housemaid, laundress, shopper. She attends to mending, discipline, entertaining and interior decoration. And every day new things are asked of her. The PTA, the church, the community center are all demanding some of her time and energy.

Often she is interrupted in her work, or she must interrupt herself in one job to go to another. In her effort to get everything done, she may not get enough rest. She may feel that she doesn't have time for social or intellectual life. She may have to neglect her talents and hobbies, or even her husband and children, because she is so busy with the physical details of keeping the house running.

Even though she loves her family and wants to do everything that will please them, she may find herself unable to cope with all the demands that her job makes.

When the family wants her to go on a picnic or a trip, she can't because too much work will be left undone at home or because getting ready and cleaning up afterward make more work than the trip is worth.

By means of scientific management she can simplify the housework so that it takes less of her time and energy and leaves her free for other activities. She can arrange her work so that it is done with more satisfaction or at more convenient times. She can interest the other members of the family so that they come to regard home management as an interesting engineering problem, and not just "mother's work."

This book will help her. Its subject is scientific management in the home. It will show the homemaker how to analyze her different jobs and see where she is being inefficient.

There are many books which give you exact instructions for making a cake or a slipcover, for cleaning a bedroom or polishing silver. This book is not like that.

A dress pattern comes with exact instructions for making one particular dress. A book on designing tells you how to make patterns. This book is like the book on designing. It will help you to understand the basic principles that underlie all kinds of jobs. Occasionally there will be repetition. That is because there is much overlapping of work principles. Like the notes of a chord, they are in effect all together, though they may be studied separately. As you study them, you will learn to think in terms of work patterns, and to bring order and beauty into your job of homemaking.

There will be profits too. The profits will be measured not in dollars and cents, however, but in family happiness.

Chapter 1

Your Goals and Your Budgets

KNOWING WHAT YOU WANT AND WHAT YOU HAVE TO GET IT WITH

Suppose that the owner of a factory—let's say a canning factory—feels that his business is not doing quite as well as it should. He calls in an engineer. The first thing the engineer has to do is to sit down with the owner and have a talk. The owner tells him what products he makes, what he hopes to add. He may say he would like to enlarge the factory, increase his output and his profits. He may think he wants to concentrate on one or two products, tomatoes and beans, for instance. Or perhaps he wants to add more products to the ones he already handles. He gives the engineers an idea of his goals, so that the engineer knows what he's working for. He also tells him what his resources are—how much labor he can employ, how much space he has, what his expenses are, so that the engineer knows what he has to work with.

In a home, you must do the same thing. It is very important for a family to know where it is going and what it is working for. With the goal in view, you are like the helmsman of a boat, keeping your eye on some object on the distant shore. If you go off your course, you can take a reef in the sail, lean on the rudder and proceed on your way again.

If you lose sight of your goal for very long, however, you are apt to find yourself going around in circles and wallowing in the trough of the waves.

Some families like to be very articulate about their goals. Others feel abashed at talking too openly. This doesn't matter as long as there is understanding and agreement among the members of the family about what the goals are. But be sure of this. Don't take too much for granted.

Of course your goals will depend on your beliefs. For example, you might say that the chief goal of the family was to achieve happiness for all its members. But happiness can be interpreted in many different ways. One family may think it consists of acquiring mink coats and convertible cars. Another may believe that it is better to put up with self-denial in the present and save its money for old age. A third may not think of happiness in material terms at all, but in terms of leisure to read or walk or join a singing society.

One parent, remembering a strict father, might think he was making his children happy by being very permissive. Another might say, "It didn't do me any harm to have to toe the line. Let them learn early that life is no bed of roses; then they won't feel the thorns so much when they grow up."

One housewife may think that the more time she spends on her home, the better she is at her job. She may feel guilty if she isn't always at it. Another may think that the faster she manages to zip through her work, the more credit she deserves. There may be truth in all of these beliefs for those who hold them. They may not be true for you.

So each family must decide on its own philosophy, and, according to its beliefs, decide what things it wants to achieve within a given span of time.

Suppose your family consists of only two—yourself and your husband. Perhaps your long-range goal is to acquire a home, to raise children, to get your degree, to continue with your profession in addition to your homemaking. Your husband's long-range goal may be to advance in his job or to fit himself for a different kind of work. You may dream of travel. You may want to study music or painting.

When you have children, your goals are multiplied. You plan for their education. You must decide what schools and camps they will go to. They may need special training for their talents, or special care for handicaps.

Then of course the children will have their own private goals.

Johnny may think he wants to be a fireman or a veterinarian. Mary may aspire to be a ballet dancer. Little Joe may long to be a cowboy. You want to help them pursue their interests, even though these interests may change from year to year.

Then there are the short-range goals. The house needs re-papering. Johnny wants a bicycle. Little Joe's teeth need fixing. You want to make a rock garden. Your husband wants to play golf or improve his bridge game (or he thinks you should improve yours). You must plan for next summer's vacation. Or perhaps this becomes a long-range goal when the family decides to work for a cottage at the lake instead of going on a two-week trip each summer.

In addition to carrying out your own plans, you must take part in the larger plans of the community. You want to be active in the doings of the PTA or the Red Cross or the local political club or the Boy Scouts.

There are chores that have to be done at different seasons, such as putting up storm windows or moth-proofing winter woolens.

Besides these things, there are all the more immediate goals to be achieved, such as simply getting the day's work done and the dinner on the table, or doing the ironing or the mending or the marketing, or perhaps even getting your hair washed and your nails manicured. How in the world can you get it all done?

If you think about all these things at once, they become so jumbled up in your head that you grow discouraged. If, on the other hand, you don't stop to think, but simply go at the tasks in a hit-or-miss fashion, you may find yourself running from one thing to another until you are exhausted—an unhappy alternative.

Is there a way out? There is. You must have a *plan.* This is the first step in solving all management problems.

You will have to have a clear statement of just what everybody in your house wants to achieve.

Call a meeting of the family—father, mother, children, if they are old enough. Children are very fond of meetings, and love parliamentary procedure. They get very good at it, too, and are quick to demand a point of order or remind a speaker that he forgot to ask for the floor. Elect a secretary to keep notes of the meeting.

However, if your family doesn't want to hold a meeting, make some notes yourself.

These are not yet plans. They are really only desires. It's as if you were starting to make a list for your Christmas shopping by putting down everything you would like to buy, regardless of whether you could afford it or not.

This is a good time to invest in two notebooks—a large looseleaf one with divisions for different subjects, and a small one for your purse, to jot down memos when you are out.

On the first page of your large notebook make a list of your family's goals. Write down everything you all want to do. You will eliminate later; but for now let us see what your heart's desire is. It will not be as simple as that of the factory owner whom we mentioned earlier. He probably merely wants to make a good product and sell it at a profit. You want to achieve as much happiness and satisfaction for all the different members of your family as possible.

It is up to the housewife to be the leader in these matters. Even if she can't always get her family to talk, she can feel what they want and need. If one child wants to make ship models, she can help him fix up a work place where the other children won't disturb him. If another child wants to be in a class play, Mother can give her chances to recite before the family, so she won't be shy before a larger audience.

And now that you have made a list as long as your arm, how are you going to get these things? Like the engineer, you must know what resources you have—how much you can spend.

Well, everybody has three kinds of resources at his disposal—money, time and energy. This is true for the housewife as well as for the factory owner and the Christmas shopper. Anything we get, unless it's given to us outright, is the product of our money, time and energy, or a combination of them. And even if it's given to us, it's the product of someone else's money, time and energy.

Of course we have other assets too. We have brains, imagination, courage, skill, determination, to mention a few. But these things can't be measured, and besides, our supply of them depends only on our natural gifts and how well we use them—it may be practically unlimited. Money, time and energy, on the other hand, are strictly measurable resources, and usually limited. So we must consider carefully how we utilize them.

The shopper, finding she hasn't enough money to buy everything on her list at the fanciest store in town, may shop around in cheaper places. This takes more of her time and energy, but spares her purse. Or she may make some of the gifts. She may knit socks for the men, and run up dainty slips on her sewing machine for the girls. This means she must know well in advance of Christmas what her needs will be, so as to have plenty of time. She must decide how to spend what she has, in order to get as much as possible of what she wants.

Each of us is constantly making similar decisions.

A decision may be made upon impulse. For instance, you may suddenly decide that since it's a beautiful spring day, you will go downtown and invest all your cash on hand in a new hat, regardless of whether there's enough to pay the insurance premium that is due next week. Or you might suddenly take a look at the living room curtains and decide that you can't stand them another minute. You're going to take them down and wash and iron them, because company is coming tonight and you won't have them see those dingy curtains—forgetting that you will be so tired by evening that you will hardly make a pleasant hostess.

A better way would be to make such decisions according to a plan. This kind of planning is called budgeting. Many books have been written about budgeting. Since it is the first step in scientific management, however, it is proper to discuss it here.

The word *budget* has been allowed to become unpopular. We may think of budget meats as the tough stringy kind that require long cooking. Budget dresses mean skimpy seams and machine-made buttonholes. Budget furniture means shiny varnish and joints that come unglued.

This is a mistake. Budgeting should mean being able to plan ahead for a good dress or a well-made chair, instead of having to buy cheap ones. It often means we can have things we scarcely dared to hope for, and at the very least it means knowing what to expect so that we can avoid rude shocks and disappointments.

Essentially, budgeting is simple. You estimate what you have, or expect to have. Then you estimate what you want to get, and you divide your resources or income up among the things you want. The resources (time, money and energy) will not always be enough to cover all the things you want. So you must classify your wants. Some of them you can't get along without, and these have to be provided for no matter what happens. Other things can be skimped, or done without altogether. You can't do all this in your head, so you must keep records.

Since money is the simplest of our assets to budget, we will start with that. There are four essential steps to be taken.

Make a division in your large notebook and label it *Budget—Money.*

Step I.

Head the first page *Income.*

On this page put down all the money you expect to have coming in for a year. (It is best to budget money on a yearly basis.)

If your income is based on a regular salary, of course this is easy. If it comes in irregular amounts and at irregular times, it is harder. Then you must be careful not to depend on either a peak or a bottom income. You may estimate on the basis of last year's income, as you do with your estimated income tax.

Step II.

On another page, write *Fixed Expenses.*

Under this heading list every fixed obligation you know you will have to meet in the course of the year: taxes, life insurance payments, social security, health insurance, pension deductions, union dues, mortgage payments or rent. The fixed expenses will vary somewhat with different families. For instance, one family will consider school tuition or payments on a car as part of their fixed expenses. Another family may classify them as things they can do without, hence not fixed expenses at all. You must decide for yourself how unchanging or inevitable an expense is before you put it in this category.

Add up these expenses. The amount you get is to be divided by twelve. Now you know how much has to be set aside each month to meet these essentials.

Some of the fixed expenses, like life insurance premiums or income taxes, fall due once a year, or perhaps quarterly. If you have conscientiously set aside the monthly portion of these expenses, you will have the full amount ready when the due date comes around. It is like paying two dollars a week into a Christmas fund. Then when Christmas comes you have a hundred dollars or so to buy nice things with. Paying the insurance premium and the income tax when they are due isn't quite as much fun as buying new dolls and bicycles for the children at Christmas, but it certainly gives you a sense of comfort and well-being to know that the money is set aside and that you don't have to scrabble for it at the last moment.

A very important fixed expense is the Emergency Fund. This is a reserve fund of money which is meant to tide you over a period of unexpected expense—illness, unemployment or some other crisis. You will have to decide on your goal with regard to this fund. You may consider a couple of hundred dollars sufficient, or you may feel that there should be enough to take care of your family for several months, if necessary. You must also decide what things the fund should rightly cover—whether to dip into it when the refrigerator gets out of order, or when a storm rips the tiles off the roof, or whether to keep it for really serious contingencies and have a separate savings account for unexpected replacements.

Step III.

Your entire income is sometimes referred to as your *gross income.* Take the sum of your fixed expenses away from the gross income and what is left is called your *net income.* This is what you have to get along with for your daily living expenses. It has to cover food, clothing, home operating expenses and transportation, including automobile maintenance; it also has to cover personal and social development, sometimes called advancement, which includes education, recreation, gifts, luxuries, allowances, medical care and savings for things that don't come out of the emergency fund.

Step III is to figure out how much you spend each year for all these things.

This cannot really be done accurately until you have been

keeping a record of your spending for a year. However, you can make an estimate now, and later see how your actual spending compares with it.

Start with *food.* You may think you spend about fifteen dollars a week for food, including meat, vegetables, groceries and meals out. (Be sure to include lunch money; it is often forgotten.)

Under *home operating expenses,* you will include gas, light, telephone, water, household help, cleaning materials, laundry, repairs to the house or furniture, and perhaps a maintenance fund for replacements of household equipment. Make a monthly and an annual estimate.

Clothing may be harder to determine. One way to do it is to make a separate inventory for each member of the family. Take yourself first. Write down in one column everything you have—how much lingerie, how many stockings, shoes, dresses, blouses, suits, coats, hats, raincoats, gloves, bags and other accessories. Then make a list of all the clothes you expect to need in the coming year, in order to build up an adequate wardrobe. Be realistic about it and don't put down three evening dresses and a Mainbocher suit unless you really intend to get them. But do include everything you need in order to be well dressed according to your own standards. Estimate the prices, find the total and divide by twelve to see how much ought to be set aside each month for your clothing.

Do the same for your husband. How many suits, coats, shirts, ties, slacks, sweaters does he own? What does he need?

Do the same for each child.

Under *automobile,* include gas, oil, upkeep, repair, garage rent.

Under *personal and social development,* include grooming, music and dancing lessons, theater tickets, gifts, books, magazines, allowances, hobbies, contributions to various causes, and medical care and drugs, unless you expect to have a very large dentist or doctor bill, in which case it might have to come out of the emergency fund, or it might be classified among the fixed expenses.

When you have added up all these expenses, you may find that they come to a good deal more than your net income! You must pare them down.

As you look at the list, you will see that some of the items are what might be called semifixed. There isn't much you can do about them. Take the food bills. You can eat out less often, or serve more fish and less meat, or bake cakes instead of buying them. You may cut down the utility bills by turning off lights and sending out post cards instead of using the phone. But in general they remain pretty much the same, unless you change your standard of living drastically.

Another set of items can be called variable. These are the ones that can be cut down, or cut out altogether, if necessary. They are different for different people. Some persons can economize on clothes, but others may have jobs that require them to dress well. Some people can dispense with an automobile. Others need a car for their work, or would feel very unhappy or deprived without one. The money you spend for sports, hobbies, theaters, gifts, books and so on, can usually be reduced. That is for you to decide.

Now you can set up a tentative budget.

Below is a sample budget as it might be set up for a family of three, with a gross income of $4800.

EXPENSES	ANNUALLY		MONTHLY	
Fixed expenses				
Federal income taxes	$500.00		$41.67	
Social security	72.00		6.00	
Life insurance	150.00		12.50	
Health and hospital insurance	72.00		6.00	
Union dues	60.00		5.00	
Rent	780.00		65.00	
Emergency fund	240.00		20.00	
		1874.00		156.17

EXPENSES	ANNUALLY		MONTHLY	
Semifixed and variable expenses				
Food	1080.00		90.00	
Clothing (including cleaning, repair and storage)	360.00		30.00	
Transportation	150.00		12.50	
Household operating expense (gas, light, phone, laundry, repairs and upkeep, help)	480.00		40.00	
Personal and social development				
Grooming	60.00		5.00	
Recreation	120.00		10.00	
Books, newspapers, gifts, etc.	120.00		10.00	
Allowances	60.00		5.00	
Hobbies	60.00		5.00	
Education	180.00		15.00	
Health	120.00		10.00	
Benevolences	60.00		5.00	
Savings	76.00		6.33	
		2926.00		243.83
TOTALS		$4800.00		400.00

You will see that in this budget no provision has been made for the purchase of new furniture, a house or any such major item. Things like this must come out of savings, if possible. For this reason some authorities classify installment payments on cars and furniture as savings, though they certainly don't look like savings because you don't put the money in the bank and also because you usually pay more for anything you buy on the installment plan.

Note that there is no allocation for a car in this budget. The maintenance of a car is expensive. If a family in this income bracket must have a car, they will have to cut down on some other items. Some will spend less for food, others will economize on household operating expenses. Or they may be forced to spend less on personal and social development. If there is an increase in the fixed or semifixed expenses, like taxes, union dues, food or rent, they may have to give up their savings account. This should only be done as a last resort.

Some of the items grouped under personal and social development should be discussed further. *Allowances* refers to children's pocket money. Some families prefer to give each member an allowance to take care of all incidental expenses such as lunch and carfare and haircuts, instead of breaking down these small expenses under food, transportation and grooming. If you do this, you will of course increase the allowance budget, and decrease those for the separate items.

The allowance for *health* is to take care of everything not covered by health insurance—drugs, eyeglasses, dentures, etc., as well as doctors' and dentists' bills.

Now that you have set up a tentative budget, you can begin to use it. First you must set aside a sum each month to cover your fixed obligations. Once you know that they are taken care of, half the battle is won. Each month put the amount agreed on in the bank or wherever you decide to keep it. Keep a separate record in your notebook of what you set aside. You may have it in the form of a chart like this:

MONTHLY SET-ASIDES

Month	Inc. Tax	Social Security	Insurances	Dues	Rent	Emergency Fund	Total
Jan.	$41.67	6.00	18.50	5.00 √	65.00 √	20.00	156.17
Feb.	$41.67	6.00	18.50	5.00 √	65.00 √	20.00	156.17
Mar.	$41.67	6.00	18.50	5.00 √	65.00 √	20.00	156.17
	$125.01 √	18.00	55.50 √			60.00	

And so on for each month. Here you can see by totaling the columns how much is in each account at any one time. Check off the items after they have been paid. If you pay your rent monthly, make a check beside the figure each time. If you pay your income tax quarterly, check it off every three months. As the emergency fund accumulates, you can see how much is in it at all times. Leave some extra space in your chart for payments that occur occasionally. You may wish to have as one of your set-asides a maintenance fund for the house or the car. Some people calculate car depreciation according to the mileage and deposit a sum in the bank each month, varying with the use of the car for the month just past. Then when the time comes to trade in the old car and get a new one, they have the money ready. If you are making payments on a car or on furniture, you might have a set-aside account for that.

Many people have their income tax, insurance and pension deductions withheld each month by their employers. If this is true for you, of course you need not include those items among your set-asides. But don't forget to enter them in your budget.

Step IV.

The next thing is to keep a record of your daily spending. You cannot really know how much should be budgeted for your variable and semifixed expenses until you have observed what you really do spend over a period of several months or a year.

There are several ways to do this. You can set up your own method or adapt one from a book on household finance. Here is a simple way to keep accounts.

Put the name of the month at the top of the page. Then rule a column for each category of expense. Allow three extra columns for date, name of item, and amount. This is how it will look:

JANUARY

Date	Item	Amt.	Food	Clothing	Transport.	House Op. exp.	Pers. & Soc.	Savings
Budget for Jan.		243.83	90.00	30.00	12.50	40.00	65.00	6.33
1	vegs.	2.00	2.00					
	suit press	1.00		1.00				
	shoes fixed	1.50		1.50				
	fare	.70			.70			
2	laundry	1.75				1.75		
	shampoo	1.00					1.00	
	meat	3.50	3.50					
	gro.	4.23	4.23					
3	milk	3.20	3.20					
	stockings	2.90		2.90				
	lamps					1.08		

And so on for the rest of the month. This is a useful budget form because it provides a reminder of just what you have spent your money on. By adding the *amount* column, you know how much you have spent altogether, and by totaling up the columns for the separate accounts you know whether you are keeping within your budget for each account. It is a good idea to add up your columns and put in the subtotals at least once a week. Then you can glance at the budget figure at the head of the column and know whether you are going to keep within it. If at the end of two weeks you find you have spent $60.00 for food, you will know you have to economize before the end of the month if you are going to keep within your monthly budget.

During the trial period, don't slip. If you have a weak memory, carry a small notebook around in your purse and jot down everything you spend.

Now after several months you can easily see how much you

have spent on each category. If you are constantly exceeding the budget figure on some expenses, then the amounts you estimated may need to be adjusted. Suppose you find that during the first three months you spent all your money, but it included nothing for clothes. You just didn't happen to need any clothes during that time. On the other hand, you spent a good deal more for food than the sixty-five dollars you estimated, and you bought theater tickets three times. Now you need a suit which cost forty dollars, and you haven't got the forty dollars. Where is the suit money to come from?

You may try to economize on food. But you probably won't be able to save any large amounts there, unless you have been in the habit of eating in restaurants a great deal. In order to set aside something every month for clothing, so that the money will be there when you need the suit, it may be necessary to retrench altogether on the theater tickets, or to do your hair at home instead of going to the hairdresser, or to spend two dollars instead of five for a gift.

Your washing machine may have served you faithfully for years, when all of a sudden it gives one last gurgle and dies. Or the sofa that you have been patching up simply can't be patched up any longer and you must have a new one. If you have been putting some money into a maintenance fund each month, you can take care of these things without too much pain. Some people would consider that an unexpected large expense might be paid for out of the emergency fund. Others would maintain that that was only for crises, like the illness of the breadwinner, or a fire, flood or tornado, and that replacements should come from the maintenance fund which is part of the home operating account.

That is something you will work out for yourself. The main thing is to have some workable plan for keeping track of your money and setting aside what will be needed for regular expenses.

You may have some trouble deciding just *where* to set it aside. Some people get a nice budget worked out on paper, and then when they go out they just spend whatever money happens to be in their purse. They can't carry the budget along with them, and if they see a good buy in men's shirts or roasting chickens, it's pretty hard to remember just which of the dollar bills they have are meant for food and clothing, and which are for other things. After a few years of household marketing, you learn to carry the figures around in your head, but at first you may have to keep the money in separate envelopes, using all your will power to avoid opening any envelope except for the account for which it is labeled.

Some people keep their various set-asides in different banks, so the money won't get mixed up: a car fund in one bank, an emergency fund in another, insurance and income tax in a third, household operating expense in a fourth. If you are good at figures and can keep books accurately, this won't be necessary. You can control the whole situation from your record book.

As to how rigid to be, that depends. If your family is made miserable by a too rigid budget, relax. But if you enjoy figures and get a feeling of security from knowing your financial standing at all times, by all means keep track of your money down to the last cent. It's a good idea to get a little pocket adding machine to help you with the arithmetic.

If you find, after keeping a budget for some time, that you are always sailing too close to the wind, and that no amount of economizing on the variable expenses seems to leave you a safe margin, it may be necessary to alter your standards somewhat. You may have to move to a less expensive neighborhood in order to cut down on rent, commutation and upkeep. You may have to cut out summer camp and arrange a cheaper vacation. You may do your own repairs on furniture and clothing, or even make these things yourself instead of paying professionals.

What you do depends on the family. Some families find the small economies hard and would rather leave the lights burning and use the phone with a lavish hand, and have fewer new clothes.

One woman would rather have only one suit but a really good

one. Another feels better with five or six inexpensive dresses in her closet.

One would get a job and have more money, and another prefers to be at home even if it means she has less of everything.

Having a job presents posers, too. You must consider whether it really pays. An extra fifty or sixty dollars a week looks good until you stop to consider that you will do one or more of the following:

Buy more good clothing.

Spend more on carfare and lunches and in other ways.

Pay a maid to do some of your work.

Buy more expensive food because it takes less time to prepare.

Eat out more often.

Use up a great deal more time and energy.

All of these things may be worth while if the job is important to you, makes you more interested in people and more interesting to your family when you are with them. But if you have small children who would suffer without you, or if you feel unhappy about leaving your home, it may be better to alter your standards rather than maintain them at too high a price.

And when you plan the changes, don't forget your goals. The idea of a budget is to make the goal an achievement—to make the dream come true. So go back to the list you made and see that the most important goals aren't overlooked.

Budgeting Time

Budgeting money is important. Budgeting time is twice as important. After all, you can get more money if you are really determined. You can't get any more time. There are twenty-four hours in the day and that's all. What you do with them is what makes your life.

You can budget time just as you do money. First you must keep some accounts to see what you really do with your day. You may say, "I have no time to read." Or, "I spend all my time on the house." Or, "The children take all my time."

Sometimes you see a woman who gets lots of things done: she teaches school, keeps house, makes her own clothes and entertains a couple of times a week. You say, "If only I had her energy!" Actually she may not have any more energy than you, but she knows how to use her time without wasting it.

A careful record of what you do with your time may give you some surprises. Maybe you really do read, snatching a few minutes or half an hour now and then in the middle of some other task. Maybe you interrupt your housework so that it takes nearly all day before the vacuuming is done. Perhaps the children are always around and don't understand that certain times are your own.

One of the first principles of using time well is to avoid interruptions. Of course this doesn't apply if you have a young baby. A baby is a law unto itself, and the biggest interrupter there is. It would be nice if you could have an emergency fund of time when the children are little, because this is when you could surely use it. However, if there are unavoidable interruptions, you should try all the more to skip the unnecessary ones.

Begin by noting in your book, on a separate page, the moment at which you arise. If you are too sleepy to focus before you have your coffee, try to remember afterward what time it was when you got up. Then go through the day jotting down the time at which you start each task. This will make a very jerky day for you, but do it anyway. In budgeting time, it is necessary to know how long any task takes, just as budgeting money requires knowing how much things cost.

If you have somebody who can follow you around and note down your use of time, so much the better. Perhaps your husband can do this on a day off; or you can draft a child who is old enough to take an interest in the project. Student teachers do this kind of thing in nursery schools. They stand around watching the children and making notes of their activities. At first the children stare at them curiously, but soon they get so used to being observed that they pay no attention.

So, if you have an assistant to help you with your time observation, learn to go on working without stopping to talk too often. Perhaps you can get a neighbor to take time off from her housework to time you at yours, and then do the same for her.

When you have timed yourself for a while, the page in your notebook may look something like this:

7:00 Wake up.
7:15 Get up, dress, wash.
7:30 To kitchen, start breakfast.
7:45 Help Mary dress. Give little Joe breakfast in high chair.
8:00 Serve breakfast to the others.
8:15 John leaves for train.
8:25 Braid Mary's hair. Help Johnny find books. Look for lunch money.
8:40 Children leave for school. Johnny comes back to find gym shoes.
8:45 Eat breakfast. Little Joe plays in room.
9:00 Dress Joe and tidy his room.
9:30 Wash dishes, straighten living room.
10:00 Put Joe outside. Talk to neighbor.
10:20 Mail comes. Look through new Sears catalogue.
10:35 Make beds. Tidy bedrooms and bathroom.
11:15 Make shopping list. Wanted to go to store but it is too late now. Read Joe a story.
11:45 Start lunch. Doorbell rings. Vacuum cleaner salesman.
12:10 Children come home. Give them lunch.
12:40 Children go back to school. Wash dishes.
1:00 Put Joe down for nap. Tell him story.
1:30 Eat lunch and read magazine.

And so on through the day until bedtime. Do it as well as you can. Don't scold yourself if you get so busy that you forget.

If you can't do it all in one day, try the morning one time and the afternoon another. Perhaps the afternoon and evening will look like this:

2:00 Joe gets up. Dress him and go shopping.
3:00 Come home. Start to iron clothes.
3:15 Older children come from school. Give them snack and send them out to play.
3:30 Go on with ironing.
3:45 Answer phone.
4:00 Doorbell rings. Fuller Brush man. Look at samples.
4:15 Iron some more.
4:30 Put away ironing board. Sit down to rest. Children come in. Help them put away coats.
5:00 Start dinner.
5:30 Telephone.
5:40 Go on with dinner preparation.
6:15 Serve dinner. (Late because of interruptions.)
7:00 Clean up and straighten kitchen.
7:45 Play with children.
8:15 Start putting Joe to bed. (He should go at 8.)
8:30 Older children to bed.
9:00 Finish ironing.
10:00 Get ready for bed.
10:30–11:15 Read in bed.

The day after, concentrate only on certain activities. For instance, see how long it takes each time you wash dishes. It has been calculated that when a woman has been married five years she has washed 135,000 dishes, taking about 75 days to do it. It would be interesting to know how many hours of your life you spend at this dreamy task. See how long it takes you actually to tidy the living room. Perhaps on some days it takes longer because you sit down to look at a magazine. See how much time you spend each day marketing, how much doing laundry, how much sleeping, cooking, serving meals, telephoning, reading; how much with the children; how much going from one place to another; how much doing nothing while you are waiting for the water to boil, for Father to come home to dinner, for Johnny to get through in the bathroom so you can give little Joe his bath.

This project will absorb many days. Don't expect to finish it in a hurry. Keep your notebook with you while you are at home and, when you are out, make notes in your little purse notebook and transfer them to the big one later.

(If you don't think this is the most fascinating occupation in the world, remember it is going to pay off quite soon in real time dividends.)

By the end of a couple of weeks, you will have some very definite ideas on the use of your time. You will see that there are certain fixed items in the time budget. These comprise sleep, personal care, food preparation, eating and cleaning up after meals, care of children, laundry, housecleaning.

Then there are variable items, such as entertaining, hobbies, sports, social and group activities and the like. These can be cut out if necessary, though life has not much spice without them.

There are emergency items, like illness, or special jobs that have to be done by some member of the family, or unexpected trips that must be made. There are spur-of-the-moment invitations and unexpected guests.

Everybody has these fixed and variable expenditures of time. Here is a chart showing the amount of time spent by urban and farm women on housework and other activities:

DISTRIBUTION OF THE HOMEMAKER'S TIME DURING THE WEEK *

Activity	Average Time Spent By 559 Farm Homemakers		410 Homemakers in Cities of 100,000 or more	
Homemaking	*Hr.*	*Min.*	*Hr.*	*Min.*
Purchasing and Management	2	10	5	29
Care of Family	3	55	9	29
Preparing meals	15	14	9	14
Clearing away meals	7	36	4	03
Cleaning and care of house	9	37	7	20
Laundering	5	16	2	54
Mending	1	34	1	24
Sewing	3	59	2	38
Other homemaking	2	19	4	35
Total homemaking time	51	40	47	9
Farm or other work	9	35	2	5
Homemaker's working week	61	15	49	14
Sleep and rest	61	36	61	05
Leisure	27	48	37	38
Personal care	5	50	8	52
Eating meals	9	13	9	34
Other activities	2	28	1	37
Average size of household (persons)	4.3		3.9	

* Unpublished data, Bureau of Home Economics, U.S. Department of Agriculture.

These figures are interesting because they show that whereas farm women and city women spent about the same amount of time at homemaking tasks (four and a half hours less for city women) the distribution is very different in several respects. City homemakers spent a lot more time on shopping, care of children, leisure and personal care, and farm homemakers spent more on preparing and clearing away meals, on laundry and on outside jobs like care of animals or gardens.

Here is a table showing how much help these same women received, from members of the family and from paid servants:

AVERAGE AMOUNT AND DISTRIBUTION OF HELP RECEIVED IN HOMEMAKING BY FARM AND URBAN HOMEMAKERS DURING THE WEEK *

Activity	Help Received by 559 Farm Homemakers		Help Received by 410 Homemakers in Cities of 100,000 or more	
	Hr.	*Min.*	*Hr.*	*Min.*
Purchasing and Management		15		13
Care of Family		38	5	55
Preparing meals	1	45	6	19
Clearing away meals	2	17	5	52
Cleaning and care of house	3	11	9	15
Laundering		41	5	13
Mending		9		12
Sewing		8		22
Other homemaking		11		30
Total help received	9	15	33	51

* Unpublished data, Bureau of Home Economics, U.S. Department of Agriculture.

These figures may not be typical of conditions all over the country, and they may not tally with yours, but it will be interesting to compare them, to see where they differ.

Actually a time budget is never as fixed as a money budget. You can always push things around if you must. However, if you skimp on the fixed items like sleep or meals or personal care, you pay for it in some way. The experienced housewife knows about how much time it will take her to prepare a meal. Depending on the menu, she is aware that to get dinner on the table at six she must go into the kitchen at four or half-past. She can, if necessary, throw a meal together in twenty minutes, but if she does this every day the nutrition of the family may suffer. So she allows plenty of time usually, and skimps when it's necessary.

But the object of the time budget is to save time without skimping or allowing any necessary activity to suffer. Suppose, for instance, that you are in the habit of taking a quick look around your kitchen every day and then going out and spending an hour marketing. This adds up to about six and a half hours a week. You could, instead, take half an hour to make a complete list, and market once a week, taking two hours to do the whole job. You would save four hours in this way, not counting the energy it takes to get dressed, go out and carry the bundles home. You might even save money by buying in larger quantities. If your object is not to save money but to save time and energy, you might market by telephone. If you are doing some additional job along with your housework, you would certainly do well to use the telephone.

Here is a word of caution. Many tasks serve more than one purpose. Some women get their exercise and air while doing their marketing. If they didn't go out for that purpose, perhaps they would stay indoors all day. They see their neighbors, talk to the tradesmen, and get a certain stimulation from the daily jaunt. If they suddenly change their habits, they must take pains to get their stimulation in some other way.

One mother who had been in the habit of taking her young son to school every morning and calling for him every afternoon was very happy when the family moved to an apartment much closer to the school. Now he could go to school alone, which would save her a lot of time and energy. After a while she found her vitality suffering from lack of sufficient fresh air.

You may have noticed that all jobs have three parts—the *get ready,* the *job* itself, and the *clean up* after the job is finished. Sometimes the *get ready* and the *clean up* take longer than the actual work. Getting out the mending basket, looking for a spool of thread, finding a button to fix Johnny's shirt and then putting all these things away again may take ten minutes. This is out of all proportion to the sewing on of one button. If all the things that need mending are put in one place when they come home from the laundry, and the mending is done at some particular time, the ten minutes can be applied to a whole basketful of clothes instead of just one shirt.

Much time can be saved by combining the *clean up* of one job with the *get ready* of another. If, while drying the supper dishes, for instance, you put on the table those needed for breakfast, you will have the table set with no extra effort.

Time can be saved by buying clothing and furnishings that don't need much care. Nylon socks for the men seldom need darning. Polo shirts for the children never need to have buttons sewed on, just as they never need to be ironed. Stainless steel tableware never needs polishing. Of course, you won't want to scrap your present possessions, but when the time comes to buy new things you should consider this point.

Time can be saved by making a study of delays and interruptions. Housework is perhaps more subject to these annoyances than any other field of human endeavor, so a certain number of them must be expected. Many, however, are unnecessary. As you analyze your records of time spent, you will see how to cut down on them. Many delays in the course of your work call for a better schedule for yourself and for your helpers so you won't be standing around with the clean curtains in your hand, for instance, waiting until Father gets through burning the rubbish and comes to help you hang them up. Make sure your tools are in good order and your supplies kept up. Then you won't have to stop work to sharpen a knife or go out for a can of floor wax which should have been ready for use.

Telephone calls, unexpected visits, arrival of delivery men or inspectors or salesmen, calls from Johnny or Mary to help them find this or that can successfully break up your day. You may find that it takes you two hours to do an hour's ironing because you haven't the courage to disregard the telephone or the doorbell. You may find yourself working in the evening when you should be resting because you can't find a clear stretch of time during the day in which to get the work finished.

Analyze your own feeling about interruptions. Maybe you really welcome them as a change from what you are doing. Maybe you have allowed the family to get into the habit of calling on you all the time because you like the sense of being needed. Of course, children like to know that Mother is at hand, but if you enlist their co-operation they can take pride in saving your time by saying, "Mother is busy, may I take a message for her?" Teach them to write down names and telephone numbers on the pad by the telephone, and to be ingenious about helping themselves instead of asking questions all the time.

Time can be saved by forming habits. If you are in the habit of getting up, doing dishes, making beds at the same time every day, you save the minutes it would take to stop and figure out what to do next. You also save the time it takes to overcome resistance. Getting started promptly, especially at something you don't much like, is a wonderful technique to acquire.

Time can be saved by the changing of standards. If the preparation for a guest means that the whole house has to be made spick-and-span, then we may say we have no time for guests. If it just means we hang out fresh guest towels, and that guests take pot luck and feel like members of the family, then we have lots of time.

Living in a separate dwelling house means that time has to be devoted to the general care of the house. There are the screens, the storm windows, the furnace, the lawn, the garbage disposal, the snow shoveling, the painting and the repairs, all to be attended to by the house owner, unless he can afford to hire someone to do these things for him. People who live in apartment houses get many of these services as part of their contract with the landlord.

When you know what activities have to go into your time budget, what has to be done in the course of the day, week or month, and how long each of them is likely to take, you can plan a tentative daily and weekly schedule.

A good way to chart it is by grouping jobs around the times set for fixed activities. Getting up, going to bed, and eating three meals a day are fixed events in most people's lives. Around them you can group the jobs of dressing, grooming, cooking, serving and tidying up. In between you are apt to have more or less long stretches of time that can be saved for other activities, jobs that have to be done at intervals, but not every day.

It is a good idea to note these on separate three-by-five cards so that you can shift them around. Have a special card for house cleaning, another for washing, another for ironing, another for shampoos, another for changing the bed linens. Estimate the time each is likely to take and note it on the card. You may put your daily schedule on cards, too, one for each day of the week, and fit the "special" cards in between the daily ones. If you are going to clean house on Monday, put the cleaning card in next to the Monday schedule. If you have an hour to spare on Tuesday, you may make several desserts. Have a card for this and clip it to Tuesday's card. Then if Wednesday is your ironing day, or the day for cleaning the cupboards, you will be able to serve a quick supper of canned foods, plus one of the extra desserts you made yesterday.

Make cards for your seasonal events, changing from summer to winter décor, canning, planting bulbs, painting, celebrating birthdays or anniversaries, things for which you want to remember to plan time. Note the date when these things should be done, and your card file becomes a reminder file to be used in connection with your date calendar.

Here is what a typical schedule might look like, whether it is written on cards or on a page in your notebook. It is for a full-time homemaker with children of school age, and possibly one still too young for school.

TIME	ACTIVITY	REMARKS
6:45–7:00	Dress and get children up.	
7:00–7:30	Prepare breakfast.	
7:30–8:00	Serve breakfast.	
8:00–8:30	Get the children completely dressed, older ones off to school. Father started to office. Start tidying bedrooms.	Bedroom work can be started while helping children.
8:30–8:45	Finish bedrooms. Take laundry to hamper. Tidy bathroom.	
8:45–9:45	Wash dishes, straighten kitchen, start lunch preparation if necessary, straighten living room.	
9:45–11:15	Special, weekly or seasonal task.	See cards.
11:15–11:45	Rest.	Outside with child if weather permits.
11:45–12:15	Prepare lunch.	
12:15–12:45	Serve lunch. Get older children started back to school.	
12:45–1:30	Put youngest child to bed for rest, clean up kitchen, start dinner preparation.	
1:30–2:00	Rest.	
2:00–2:30	Grooming and dressing.	
2:30–5:00	Special, weekly or seasonal tasks.	See cards.
5:00–6:00	Prepare dinner.	
6:00–6:45	Serve dinner.	
6:45–7:30	Wash dishes, straighten kitchen, set table for breakfast.	
7:30–8:30	Activities with family.	
8:30–9:00	Help children prepare clothes for next day, and get them to bed.	
9:00 on	Read and rest till bedtime, grooming and bed.	

You can see that a schedule like this does not mention every move you will make during the day. It charts the day, grouping the fixed jobs together so as to leave time for rest periods, recreation and special tasks. It shows where you can save time by making the *clean up* of one job a part of the *get ready* of the next. Of course it will vary from day to day. For instance, on the day when your special task is to give the living room a good cleaning, you will not have to take the time to *straighten* the room.

It is a good idea to make yourself a special schedule for jobs that vary from time to time. You keep your house clean, but you don't clean it thoroughly every day. Here is a suggested cleaning schedule which will help you remember what to do at different times:

DAILY	WEEKLY	SEASONALLY OR OCCASIONALLY
Sweep kitchen floor	Wash kitchen floor	Wash and wax kitchen floor
Wipe range, sink, woodwork, refrigerator	Thoroughly clean range, sink, cupboard, refrigerator	Defrost and empty refrigerator, rearrange cupboards
Empty waste paper and refuse cans	Thoroughly clean refuse cans	
Tidy household	Straighten drawers and closets	Thoroughly clean drawers and closets
Tidy bathroom and wipe up spills	Thoroughly clean bathroom	Clean medicine closet, discard old medicines, clean linen or other closets in bathroom
Run carpet sweeper	Vacuum rugs and upholstery, spot clean	Thoroughly clean rugs and upholstery or have them cleaned
Dust mop floors Dust furniture Dust ornaments	Vacuum floors and baseboards, vacuum draperies and blinds, polish mirrors, silver metals, furniture	Vacuum wall coverings, clean storage cabinets, wash and wax blinds, launder curtains, clean draperies and slip covers

When you get your time budget balanced you find you have time for lots of things which once seemed just a nice dream. You can read. You can play with the children. You can rest—something too many homemakers forget. You won't feel like the old woman who got up on Monday morning and said, "Oh, dear! Today's Monday, tomorrow's Tuesday, next day's Wednesday, half the week's gone and nothing's done yet!"

You'll have confidence in your ability to get things done in their proper time.

Budgeting Energy

Energy is the capacity for performing work. It is the only one of the three main resources which comes from within the worker himself, and it is rather difficult to measure. It would not be easy for you to keep your own accounts of the energy you use mopping the kitchen floor or scrubbing the bathtub. It can be measured, of course, but usually in the laboratory or factory. If you have ever had a basal metabolism test, you will understand how energy is measured. The person being tested is given oxygen to breathe through a tube. The amount of oxygen she uses while resting is measured. This shows how much energy she needs for the processes of breathing and circulation and whatever other activities go on automatically in the body. The result is given in terms of calories.

A calorie is the amount of heat necessary to raise the temperature of one gram of water one degree centigrade, so when we say that a tablespoonful of honey has 100 calories, we mean the honey will give that much energy for the body to use.

Now when a person is doing some active work, of course she is using a lot more calories than when she is lying flat on a couch. Here is a table showing the amount of energy expended per hour under different conditions *:

* H. C. Sherman and C. S. Lanford, *Essentials of Nutrition,* Macmillan Company, New York, 1940, p. 77.

FORM OF ACTIVITY	CALORIES PER HOUR FOR EACH POUND OF BODY WEIGHT	PER CENT OF INCREASE OVER LYING STILL
Awake, lying still	0.50	
Sitting at rest	0.65	30
Standing relaxed	0.69	38
Walking 2.6 miles per hour	1.30	160
Walking 3.75 miles per hour	1.95	290
Walking downstairs	2.36	372
Walking upstairs	7.18	1336

Housework has been classified according to how much energy it requires. Light work increases the calories used by less than 100% above resting; moderately heavy work by 100% to 150%; heavy work by 150% to 200%; very heavy work by 200% to 300%; and extremely heavy work by 300% or more.*

Sweeping a rug with a vacuum cleaner with no brush requires 102.3% above resting; sweeping it with a broom, 329%.

Ironing napkins with an electric ironer requires 45%; with an iron, 70% to 80%.

And you can see that walking upstairs is one of the most strenuous things you can do.

Each person has a very definite amount of energy, and with experience we learn what its limits are and how to avoid overdrawing our account. Very young people often don't know this. They have so much energy that they are surprised to discover that it can be used up. Once in a while they do use it up. They dance all night, or clean the whole house in one fell swoop, and the next day they feel as if they had been run through a wringer. This is known as "learning the hard way." When you have learned, you are said to have "common sense."

Energy is best budgeted in connection with time. You can do

* V. W. Swartz, *The Human Energy Cost of Certain Household Tasks*, Washington Agr. Exp. Sta. Bull. 282, 1933.

so much light work in a given amount of time, rather less moderately heavy work, and still less very heavy work.

Here is a table showing how some different kinds of housework have been classified *:

LIGHT WORK	MODERATELY HEAVY WORK	HEAVY WORK	EXTREMELY HEAVY WORK
Hemming	Dusting	Sweeping floor	Sweeping rug with broom
Knitting	Using carpet sweeper	Washing clothes by hand	
Crocheting	Using some vacuum cleaners	Rinsing clothes	
Darning	Polishing floors	Wringing clothes with hand-power wringer	
Hand sewing	Dressing infant	Hanging clothes from basket on floor	
Sewing on motor-driven machine	Washing dishes		
Paring potatoes	Kneading dough		
Ironing napkins	Breadmaking		
Beating batter	Sewing by footdriven machine		
Using vacuum cleaner on rug	Wringing clothes by hand		
	Wringing clothes with electric wringer		
	Drying clothes in extractor		
	Putting up and removing clothesline		
	Hanging clothes from utility table		
	Emptying washing machine		
	Cleaning laundry equipment		
	Ironing towels		

How much you can do in a given amount of time depends not only on the heaviness of the work but on your working pace. If you don't go too fast, you can keep on longer. A runner has his pace by means of which he can trot for miles without getting exhausted. If you have to speed up, you can do it for a limited time. Your body will pour out more adrenalin and sugar to give you the necessary energy for the emergency. In case of a prolonged emer-

* P. Nickell and J. M. Dorsey, *Management in Family Living,* John Wiley and Sons, Inc., New York, 1950, p. 130.

gency such as an illness or an extra job, you may have to take steps to reinforce your energy by means of extra food, stimulants, vitamins or a tonic.

Of course, the best stimulant to energy is happiness. You know how much you can do when you are interested in the job, or when you are doing it for someone you love, or when the reward is something you want very much, or when the conditions of work are pleasant. Our industrial engineer knows that, too, and he suggests to the owner of the plant the installation of green plants, pleasant lighting, soft music and polite language. He is interested in getting people who like each other to work together. He advocates bonuses for especially good work.

Everybody knows how much the well-adjusted person can do, and how little the unhappy, tense, angry person accomplishes. The reason for this is not only that happiness increases energy, but that anger and unhappiness use up so much energy that an unhappy person has really only a small part of his strength to devote to the job. It is well, therefore, in budgeting energy, to know what things make you unhappy or angry or fearful, and to try to circumvent them.

If you find, while scrubbing the bathtub, that you are annoyed at your husband who went off and left the ring in the tub, or if you feel cross with Johnny for leaving his room in such a mess, you will get more tired than if you think of these jobs as your rightful work. You should try to make your family see how you feel about it. But try to see how they feel about it, too. If your husband won't scrub the tub, maybe you could get him to take showers instead. If Johnny won't keep his room in order, maybe a new arrangement of the room would make him more willing.

There are fixed items in the energy budget as well as in the time and money budgets. Personal care heads the list. Care of clothing, house cleaning, preparation of meals, and care of children are also very important. Some of these things take more energy at one time than at another. When the children are little, for instance, they need to be scrubbed and dressed and taken to the park. When they get bigger, child care becomes more a matter of calling after them as they go out the door, "Remember your rubbers and don't be home too late."

Then you may find that you aren't using all of your energy. Energy is meant to be used, and when it isn't, it accumulates in the form of fat, which is much harder to get rid of than money in the bank. You may have to use up extra energy by getting a job or doing volunteer work of some kind.

This warning extends also to the labor-saving devices we are so eager to have. Washing machines and dish washers are fine, but the housewife thus freed sometimes finds she isn't getting enough exercise. She has planned how to save her energy but she hasn't planned what to do with it. Savings are meant to be spent.

Of course some of the things you will spend your savings on will be the variable uses of energy. These are the hobbies, sports, picnics and parties, the church work, club attendance and creative work that make life more exciting and interesting.

When you plan activities for your time schedule, you must consider how much energy these activities take. You may figure that you have *time* for three dinner parties in one week in addition to all your housework, but perhaps you will be too tired. You may know that you have three hours free in the afternoon, which is plenty of time to set out all the tulip bulbs or spray the winter clothes. But those are hard jobs, and perhaps you would do better to work only two hours at either one of them, and spend the other hour doing the mending, which is light work. Then you can do the rest of the planting or spraying tomorrow. You may wish you could afford theater tickets. So you take a part-time job which earns you some extra money. Now you can afford the tickets, but you can't go to the theater too often because you must go to bed early and conserve your energy for the job.

In planning your work, be careful to leave space in the energy budget for family and social relations. It is often a temptation to neglect these. The children will be much more likely to remember it if you play checkers with them or read them stories than if you merely bake cakes and keep their clothes washed and ironed. And you yourself are more likely to remember the pleasant evenings of bridge or talk with your neighbors and friends than hours spent waxing the floors or running the washing machine.

Of course, you may say that if you had a full-time maid as the Joneses do, you could have a spotless home and entertain, too. But the whole purpose of the budget is to help you get along with what you have in terms of energy, time and money. If you can do that, there is sure to be satisfaction in the home. If you overdraw your accounts, the simplification of work and the better use of time and energy will help you to balance your budgets and provide peace of mind and satisfaction in living.

Chapter 2

Questions

When you have thought about your goals, and studied your budgets for money, time and energy, you are in a position to make a few comparisons. You can see whether you are really achieving your goals, or whether you are falling by the wayside.

Suppose you find that you are not accomplishing all the things you planned. And yet the jobs you are doing take all your time and use up all your energy, and you are already spending as much money as you think you can afford.

How can you get more done?

By becoming more efficient. And the first step toward efficiency is study.

Like the engineers who started by studying the work habits of bricklayers and coal shovelers, you must study the ways in which your motions and time are used, as well as the materials and the tools you work with, to find better ways of doing your work.

This is *motion and time study*.

The engineer who is going to help the factory owner increase his output or decrease his expenses will first make a motion and time study of the work methods used in the factory. He will begin by going into the factory and observing what is being done. He makes notes and asks questions. What job is each worker doing?

Why is he doing it? Is it necessary? Could he do it in some other way or in some other order or in another place? Is he the right person to do the job or would it be better to delegate some other worker to do it?

These questions are very important. In fact, you may consider them the most important part of this book. The questioning attitude is the scientific attitude and is the root of all progress, since it takes nothing for granted, but is always on the lookout for more and better knowledge.

Make a new division in your notebook. Label it QUESTIONS. Now rule off the page into six vertical columns, one for each question.

WHAT?

The first question will be WHAT. Into this column will go the name of a job—the answer to the query: what job is being done?

At first glance this may seem to be a simple question. But really it is not so simple. It is worth while to classify and name a job. In industry there are so many different kinds of jobs that a large book has been published, entitled, *Dictionary of Occupational Titles,* the purpose of which is to define jobs.

When you have named and described a job, you will have a better understanding of its limits. You will know where each job begins and ends. A job like cleaning, for instance, that seems like a major operation, falls into proper perspective when broken down into its separate parts—dusting, polishing, vacuuming, scrubbing.

When you examine each individual job to see how you can improve it, you will have units of work that are not so big as to be unwieldy. And you will also have a useful tool for teaching or delegating work to others, as you shall see later.

When you think about the many and various things that you do, you will see that the work of your home falls into several main categories:

1. Care of house
2. Care of clothing
3. Food preparation
4. Care of children
5. Personal care
6. Social activities

These main categories break down into separate activities. Care of the house means cleaning, repair, replacement (shopping), construction (building furniture, making shelves and slip covers), and storage (putting away winter things and getting out summer ones).

Care of clothing means sewing, mending, laundry and cleaning of clothes.

Food preparation means marketing, storing, cooking, serving and dishwashing.

Care of children means a variety of physical, mental and emotional activities: bathing, dressing, feeding, amusing, teaching, loving, disciplining, nursing.

Personal care consists of daily and weekly grooming, bathing, dressing, exercise, visits to doctor and dentist, and everything else that you do to keep yourself in good condition.

Then the jobs break down into still more detail. Take just one aspect of clothing care—laundry. This consists of sorting, washing, hanging out, taking in, sprinkling, ironing and putting away.

To begin your chart, take a simple job. It is well to start with one that is done frequently and that is fairly mechanical. Let us take bedmaking as a first example.

WHY?

The second column on the QUESTIONS page of your notebook will be labeled WHY, or, IS IT NECESSARY? In other words, why do this particular job at all? This question is a great timesaver.

For instance, is it necessary to make beds? Necessary means

unavoidable. Of course you could avoid making beds by just leaving them unmade all day, and climbing back into them when night came. This might suit ten-year-old Johnny well enough, but it would probably make his mother unhappy. Why? Because she finds it more comfortable to sleep in a smooth bed, because the spread keeps the dust off the blankets and sheets, and because a neatly made bed is part of the décor of the house. These are her standards, which are based on her belief that that is the best way to keep house.

When we decide what is necessary, we have to take our standards and our beliefs into account. Many things are done because that is the way we were brought up, or because that is the custom in our family or our community or our circle of friends.

People need customs as plants need roots. It is good for us to know that "this is how we do things." It gives us security. That is why we cling so hard to customs, especially in the home.

If it is Mrs. Brown's habit to make the beds right after breakfast, and if it is her belief that nobody, entering her house at ten in the morning, should ever find her with the beds unmade, then it will make her very unhappy to have to leave them so.

"It isn't right," she will say. And most of us will agree that it certainly isn't right to make a habit of leaving the beds unmade. We think a tidy, well-ordered home is essential to good family life. We think children should be raised to like order and neatness.

But it should be possible not to be too rigid about neatness. Sometimes it becomes necessary to leave the beds unmade, and then Mrs. Brown should be able to do it without too much grief. The appearance of a house is important. Mrs. Brown, however, may go to still further lengths and make life miserable for anybody who sits or lies on a bed once it is made. We might say she overvalues appearance. After all, a house is meant to be lived in, not just looked at.

Some housekeepers feel that it doesn't much matter what the décor is like, so long as everybody is comfortable. They put dark spreads on the beds so that people can lie down whenever they wish.

Other people don't think a formal bedroom is necessary at all, but prefer sitting rooms with studio couches. Still others prefer a hammock or a sleeping bag, or, as in Bali, just a mat on the floor.

The way you run your home depends on your *standards,* and your standards should be based on what you believe. If you and your family believe that you should all sit down together at breakfast, then that constitutes a standard, and that is what the family ought to do. If you believe that linen napkins should be used and that boys should wear coats at dinner, then these things are part of your standards and are necessary to you.

Here we get the clue to that sixty-four dollar question, Is it necessary? If it would lower your standard not to do certain things, then these things are necessary.

But standards can be changed. A family may decide that paper napkins do the job just as well as linen ones. The boys may feel more at ease without their coats, and be allowed to leave them off.

Maybe your standards have been too high. Take an example from the automobile industry. In English-made cars, all parts are perfectly finished. American engineers have found that some parts will function just as well if they are not so highly machined. Costs are cut down by this method, though the cars are no less efficient.

Likewise in the home, that fussy housewife, Mrs. Brown, may be insisting that floors have to be scrubbed by hand, or that the beds have to be completely stripped each morning, or that a cake must always be made from scratch. If she thought about it, she might find that she could run her house just as well by using a self-wringing mop, or by not stripping the beds, or by using cake mixes occasionally.

Ways of doing things can be changed without lowering standards.

Hot running water may be used for washing dishes, giving just as good results as the old two-dishpan method.

Canned baby food saves hours of preparation and is just as good for the baby as freshly cooked vegetables. In fact, it may be better, for the companies that prepare it are careful to use only the choicest vegetables with high vitamin content and low spray residues. One of these companies recently announced that there was evidence that babies stored DDT in their bodies, and though this might not be harmful, still the company was taking no chances, and had been obliged to destroy some carloads of food that contained too much DDT.

Store-bought food, prepared under scientifically controlled conditions, may often be better than that prepared at home, though it has long been the custom for many people to insist that they would never serve ready-made foods because their mothers didn't.

Standards may be deliberately lowered for certain occasions.

If young and inexperienced workers take over a task, we may have to be tolerant of the results. For example, if young Johnny and Mary undertake to get breakfast on Sunday morning, you won't complain if the cereal is a little lumpy or the toast a little burned, though this doesn't mean that the cereal and toast standard is going to be lowered from now on.

Maybe your standards have required that all the bric-a-brac in your house shall be dusted daily. But with the arrival of a new baby you haven't time for bric-a-brac. Either you will reduce the amount of dusting, or put away some of the bric-a-brac.

Maybe you have always insisted that meals should be eaten in the dining room. But on days when you are busiest, dinner can be served in the kitchen, or buffet style, on trays in the living room.

When there is illness in the family, you will relax your standards, make up a bed on the sofa, serve "quickie" meals, make allowances for a fussy patient's requests.

Don't be afraid of lowering standards if necessary. It is not lowering so much as failing to maintain standards that constitutes a threat. Ask yourself, "Is this suitable? Is it appropriate? Will it influence our habits? Will it make our memories happier or unhappier? Will it spoil our aesthetic satisfaction?"

For instance, does it matter how carefully the table is set, as long as it's just the family and no company? If you decide it does matter, you'll keep on setting the table carefully, even though it means more work.

Standards can be raised. You can use machines that do the job better, and yet decrease work: dish-washers, washing machines, vacuum cleaners, mixers. Standards can be raised in one department by saving time, money or energy in another. For instance, you may be able to improve your standard of dressing by making your own clothes. You will have prettier dresses than you could buy for the money you have to spend, but you will need lots of time which will have to be taken from other activities like cooking and ironing.

Standards can be changed as new problems arise. Here the family has to be consulted to see if the standard really should be changed or if you should be stricter about maintaining the old standard. For example, books are loaned and not returned. Should loaning be discontinued, or should you devise better ways of getting books back? There is a new television set in the house and visiting children forget to go home. Should invitations cease, or should we make a rule about the hours when viewing should take place? Mother wants to do some extra work at home, which means she can't spend time playing with the children in the afternoon. Shall she give up the work, or shall the children take care of themselves?

In industry and business, suggestions for changes are always welcome. There is an orderly way of doing this, known as proposal making. Maybe your family will be pleased if you prepare small sheets of paper or cards as forms for this purpose, with spaces for the existing method of doing a job, the reason for changing, and the new method proposed. Have a suggestion box, and make the proposals the subject of a family meeting.

Of course there are lots of things you don't want to change.

You may keep on doing things because you like to, and because you have always done them. You may give a party just because you feel like it. You may use doilies and finger bowls and candles just because you enjoy the air of elegance they give to your table, even though they mean more work.

Much of the past is good and should be kept. But know why you are doing it. Don't say it's because the thing *has* to be done, when really you're only doing it from habit.

You may think Monday has to be wash day. That used to be the custom. But if you take your laundry to the launderette on the corner, you may find less of a crowd there on some other day. If you have your own washer, it may be convenient to pop a few things in two or three times a week rather than have a big load on Monday.

Maybe when you were a child it was customary for the boys to mow the lawn and shovel the walks, and for the girls to help with the cooking and sewing. But really there is no reason why Mary shouldn't mow the lawn if she likes the exercise, or why Johnny shouldn't make a batch of fudge or pancakes.

You may do a thing because some one person in the family likes it—invite certain guests, or make a special pudding. You may do something because of its educational value. A puppy in the house may be an awful nuisance, but you have it because of its importance to the children.

You do something because it satisfies a group. It's good for the family to get together and build a ping-pong table or braid a rug, though it does make a bit of a mess.

You do something because it's a neighborhood custom, like having the Scout troop meet at your house, or baking cookies for a church supper.

You do something because it's a game. Perhaps you used to make a game of the dish-washing; but, now that you have a dish-washing machine, what will supply the reason for the family to get together companionably? You may have to think up another project for them—maybe building a playroom or planting a garden or having a game of canasta in the evening—in order not to lose the satisfaction that comes from group activity.

The main thing, when you ask, Is it necessary? is to know what you really think and what your standards really are. A standard doesn't imply perfection. It means the best that can be had, given the materials and conditions that exist.

And now to return to our bedmaking.

WHEN?

When should the beds be made? This is the next question. Most housewives carry their schedules about in their heads. They know almost unconsciously, for instance, that as soon as husband and children have left in the morning, they will start making the beds. This is because unmade beds give a house an untidy look, and so for quick clean up, bedmaking is the first step. There are other housewives who operate on no schedule at all, and put their hand to whatever the eye happens to light on. Sometimes they do the beds first, sometimes the dishes.

Now look at the time budget you made a while ago. You spend about four hours a week making beds. Be sure you do it when it is most convenient to you, even if it means changing your usual hour.

First, do the job when *get ready* and *clean up* can be combined with other jobs. For instance, if you do your downstairs work first, and then go up and do everything that needs to be done upstairs, you will save climbing stairs, carrying tools and moving furniture. Second, co-ordinate the activity with other things that happen. If the laundry man comes on Tuesday, let that be the day you strip the beds and air the blankets and vacuum the mattresses. And as long as you have the vacuum cleaner in the bedroom, let that be the day you vacuum the rest of the upstairs while airing the bedding.

But if you prefer to do the cleaning on Friday, perhaps you can arrange to have the laundry man come on that day, so you won't have the bundle of laundry lying about until the following Tuesday.

The question WHEN? really means two things. First, it means when in the course of time—calendar when. Second, it means when in the sequence of things.

Thus, beds are made every day in calendar time; after kitchen and living room clean up in sequence time. If other people are to help you, the time may have to be changed. If a maid is coming in, she will perhaps make the beds later. If Johnny and Mary are to make their beds before they go to school they must get up in time to do this.

Other activities come at regular or irregular intervals. The important thing is to know when they come in relation to each other and to have them planned long enough in advance so you don't have to rush to get things done, or omit them because you didn't allow time for preparation.

As you question each job that you do, you may find reason to change your time schedule. Keep it handy, either on your desk or thumb-tacked on the bulletin board. Keep your daily reminder cards there, too, and don't hesitate to add to them as you get ideas, or tear them up when you don't need them any more.

A bulletin board is a good communications center. Put up reminders, advance notices and instructions, and train your family to look there for information and to leave notes for you of any plans they have.

As an adjunct to the bulletin board, have a big calendar on the kitchen wall, with enough space around each number to write in the engagements, duties and plans of each member of the family. It helps to see a month all at once.

WHERE?

The next question for you to ask is, Where shall this job be done? With beds the answer is obvious; with other activities not always so.

Clothes may be sorted in the bathroom where they are taken out of the hamper, or in the cellar or kitchen where the washing machine is kept. This may mean carrying the sheets and other things that are sent out to the kitchen and then back again. Perhaps you can save sorting by having several receptacles—a bag for socks, a separate hamper for linen, a lined hamper or bag to keep your nylons and lingerie from snagging.

The vegetables may be prepared on the porch or in the garden to keep refuse out of the house, or even in the living room (shelling peas, for example), if you have that kind of living room.

The baby can be bathed in the kitchen instead of the bathroom.

Lunch can be eaten in the bedroom off a tray to keep a sick child company, or in the living room before the TV set.

What matters is your convenience, not convention.

HOW?

This question really requires a chapter all to itself. HOW refers to the method of doing a job, and improving the method requires plenty of careful study. It will be discussed more fully in a later chapter. For the present, simply put down in a few words your present way of doing the job.

WHO?

In a home that is democratically run, everybody does his share. In some homes this means: Father brings in the money, the children go to school and play, Mother does the greater part of the housework, and each member of the family at times does certain household jobs. Father may clean the furnace, put up shelves and screens and storm windows. The boys do outdoor jobs and heavier work like mowing the lawn, shoveling snow, stoking the furnace, washing the car, chopping firewood. The girls help Mother by washing dishes, dusting, making beds, cooking.

This is the conventional division of tasks, based on the premise that girls should be trained to do all household chores except those requiring the superior strength of men and boys.

Nowadays, lines are not drawn so sharply. Fathers may wash dishes and take care of babies, mothers have jobs outside the house, girls wash cars and boys make hamburgers.

So, division of labor in the home should be based on two questions. First, is this the best person to do the job? Second, is this person learning something or getting some special satisfaction from doing the job?

The housewife may be the best person to make the beds five days a week. Maybe on Saturday she has extra cooking to do, and on Sunday she should rest and read the Sunday paper, so on those days the children make their own beds. Besides, children should learn to make beds and do other chores, first, so they will not be helpless when faced with them, and second, because we want them to have respect for work, a willingness to do it cheerfully, and a feeling of being contributing members of the family and not parasites. How they *feel* about it is the important thing, and their attitude toward work will be modeled on yours.

It may very well be that Mother is not the best person to make the beds the other five days either. If she doesn't enjoy the work, but can write a story or do some typing that will pay enough to hire help, then that is a more economical and satisfying way to arrange it.

You should know the money value of your time. There is an old-fashioned feeling that woman's time at home has no money value. This is because she doesn't actually get wages. To get a true picture of the value of your services, try computing how much you would have to pay a maid to come in and do all your work. At the rate of a dollar an hour, eight hours a day (and most homemakers work more than eight hours), seven days a week, this comes to fifty-six dollars, not counting carfare and meals.

There may be many reasons why you don't want to go out to work. Still, if you can earn money at home without paying for overhead like extra clothes and carfare, you may be justified in hiring help, or sending out such work as laundry, cleaning and clothes repair, or even sending the children to a play group.

As much as possible, unless there is some educational reason, apportion jobs as they are apportioned in industry, that is, according to the abilities, the needs, and the desires of the workers. For instance, if Johnny loves pets, let one of his tasks be to feed and care for the dog, the turtles and the goldfish. This may compensate for some of the jobs he doesn't like, such as dishwashing. If Mary likes to shop, let her do some of the marketing or buying of clothes. Give responsibility (but don't force it).

To develop good attitudes, work together on a job, even though it means you aren't really being relieved of it. If Johnny resists making his bed, you may have to say, "Come on, let's do your room now," and help him with it, more for the sake of the company than the actual work.

People will work if there is a reward in view. For you the reward of bedmaking or dishwashing is the satisfying sight of a tidy bedroom or a closet full of clean dishes. To Johnny those don't mean much. But he may feel rewarded by the satisfaction of trying a new job, or of relieving someone else of a job that is hard, or of freeing someone to do something that pleases him (as when he minds the baby so that Mother can sew his Hallowe'en costume) or of working in a group.

Now, after all this soul-searching, we can complete our bedmaking chart. It will look something like this:

WHAT?	IS IT NECESSARY?	WHEN?	WHERE?	HOW?	WHO?
CARE of beds	Yes	After breakfast except on Fri. Then after airing	—	Air on Fri. Change sheets Vac. mattress & springs once a month	Mother Mon. through Fri. Mary & Johnny make beds Sat. & Sun.

If you are satisfied with this analysis, call it the *standing order* for bedmaking. This is the term used in industry.

Post it on your bulletin board, or keep it handy in your notebook, but remember that it is not meant to be permanent, but only to remain until you think up a better way of doing the job.

Now let us analyze another activity, say ironing.

If you were suddenly asked, "Is ironing necessary?" you might at once say yes. But if you think about it you will see that this is not the whole answer. There are many different kinds of clothes. Should they all be ironed? Some should, others shouldn't.

For example, it is absolutely necessary to iron a man's cotton office shirt. It can't be worn unironed. Your husband might not get arrested if he went to the office in rough-dry shirts, but he might have trouble keeping his job.

On the other hand, pajamas and shorts can be used unironed, especially if they have been hung and folded carefully. This is a matter of your standards. Some people can be happy with their underwear or sheets folded but not ironed. Others would feel they were living on Tobacco Road.

One way to get around this difficulty is to buy clothes and linens that aren't meant to be ironed—things made of seersucker, terry cloth, jersey, balbriggan, nylon tricot. Some nylon shirts for men need only a light pressing with a warm iron. Others can be hung up wet and need not be ironed at all.

You can use things that don't even need to be washed. In addition to paper napkins, there are tissues instead of handkerchiefs, paper tablecloths and hand towels, paper dish towels and dusters, disposable diapers. There are plastic cloths and mats and bibs and aprons that can be wiped clean with a damp cloth.

There are paper curtains which are so cheap that they can be thrown away when dirty without compunction. Some people look forward to paper clothes which will be soft enough and sturdy enough for comfort, and yet cheap enough to discard.

Having decided which things must be ironed, you must now

decide which need to be dampened. Some nylons don't. Flannelettes don't. Some washing machines take so much water out of the clothes that you need only lay them out on a table for an hour or so and then iron, thus skipping the hanging up, the taking down and the dampening. This may mean a change in your sequence, since you must plan to iron before the things get dry—or before they mildew.

Now come the questions, WHEN, WHERE, HOW.

Suppose you are accustomed to ironing in the morning, in the kitchen, standing up at the ironing board, walking across the room with each freshly ironed piece to hang it on a rack.

Perhaps it might be better for you to iron in the living room or the bedroom, where there is more light and air; in the afternoon, when you can listen to a radio program that you want to hear, or when the children are home from school so that you can hear Mary read or help Johnny with his spelling; and sitting on a stool with your basket of sprinkled clothes at your left hand, and the rack within reach at the right so that you need not get up at all. You would probably get done faster, be less tired, and accomplish more.

But you would have to make some adjustments in your work habits. This might not seem hard to you. But you would be surprised to know how many women resist such changes. They give all sorts of reasons. "It looks lazy to sit down." "I'm used to ironing in the kitchen." "I don't get enough pressure on the iron unless I stand up." "I just have to get my work done in the morning."

Some of these beliefs carry over from the days when we had to heat our flatirons (sadirons, they were aptly called) on the coal or wood stove. The iron didn't remain hot long, and had to be changed frequently. So the worker had to stay in the kitchen where the stove was. But the stove was so hot that she couldn't stand very near it, so she walked back and forth to get her hot irons when she needed them. The old irons required a lot of pressure. Standing made it easier to bear down hard. But now those irons have been given a coat of bright paint and relegated to the position of door-stops. Modern electric irons have controlled heat and can be plugged in anywhere. So why not change your habits?

Let us say your ironing chart originally looked like this:

WHAT?	NECESSARY?	WHEN?	WHERE?	HOW?	WHO?
Ironing all clothes	Yes	Tues. A.M. after clean-up	Kitchen	Sprinkle after breakfast. Iron. Hang on rack	Mother

Now after deciding on some changes, you can make a new chart below the old one. It might look like this:

WHAT?	NECESSARY?	WHEN?	WHERE?	HOW?	WHO?
Ironing	Blouses Dresses Suits Pajamas Handker-chiefs	Wed. after-noon	Bedroom	Sprinkle all but pajamas. Sit on stool. Basket at left. Rack at right Send shirts out	Let Mary do hand-kerchiefs

Now you try out the new way. If it works, good. Let this be your standing order. If it doesn't work, keep on trying other changes until you hit on something that does.

Now go and chart more activities. Take your time schedule and go down the list and analyze every job—or as many as you can, putting the most thought into those you do most often. If you don't wish to put it all down on paper, do it mentally. As you work, question. Am I doing this at the right time? Am I the right person to do it? Could I change my work place?

If you get new ideas, make a note of them, and the next time you do the job, do it the new way. Give yourself time to plan, since the first time you use the new method the *get ready* and *clean up* may take longer. Later, when the whole task becomes habitual, you hope it will take much less time.

And when you post the new standing order, be sure to listen

to the family's comments about it. You want to be sure it's easily understood and accepted by those who may have to do the job.

If they say, after a fair trial, "I don't understand this," or "Do I *have* to do it this way?" or "It sounds too complicated," or "It's boring," you know a rewrite is indicated.

Chapter 3

Motionmindedness

How did engineers ever get the idea of simplifying work by means of motion study? They did not really invent anything new. Their contribution was more in the nature of a discovery. Sir Isaac Newton did not invent the law of gravitation, but discovered it when the apple hit him on the head, as the legend has it. In like manner the engineers simply observed the ways in which certain people worked, and then systematized them. Let us see what this means.

A housewife who is trying to keep within her financial budget finds ways of making short cuts. She can rejuvenate an old hat with new trimming, or dress up a meat loaf dinner with a fancy dessert. Some people are gifted that way.

Other people have a natural gift for budgeting energy. They see work in terms of short cuts. We say that they are *motion-minded.*

In any kind of repetitive job, they form patterns of work. They use both hands effectively. They arrange their work places so that their tools are within reach and permit the best sequence of motions. Their eyes are ahead of their hands, planning the next move. Their co-ordination is good.

They may behave in this way without realizing it, because it comes naturally to them. But even people who don't have this natural gift can improve their work methods by thinking about them and observing motionminded people.

The engineer going into the canning factory takes particular note of the way in which different workers go about their jobs. He can often get good ideas that way.

For instance, two women may be peeling tomatoes. One will walk to the table where the unpeeled tomatoes are, take a tomato, walk back to the sink and peel it, reach over to put it into a big kettle, and then, dripping tomato juice on the floor from her wet hands, walk back to the table for another tomato.

Another woman has arranged things differently. She has a stool in front of the sink. She puts a basket of unpeeled tomatoes at her right, a pan to catch the peelings in front of her, and another pan for the peeled tomatoes at the left. She sits on the stool. Her only movements are those which her hands and arms make in taking a tomato from the right, peeling it and putting it at the left. When she gets near the bottom of the basket, she may notice someone walking near the supply table.

"Oh, Anna," she says, "while you're on your feet, bring me some more tomatoes."

She is motionminded. She plans her work. Instead of walking back and forth with one or two tomatoes, she arranges her work place so that most of her body is resting while both hands work rhythmically from right to left. Her eyes watch the progress of the work. Her mind is quick to take advantage of available help.

By the end of an hour she has much more work done and is not half so tired as her unmethodical co-worker.

Of course, you might say that the friend likes to walk back and forth, so why shouldn't she? If she likes it, all right. There are many people who have so much energy and are so fond of using it that they walk back and forth with each dish as they dry the dishes, they clear tables carrying one plate in each hand instead of using trays, they run up and down stairs at the slightest provocation. For such people, sitting or standing still and reducing their motions is punishment.

Most people who are wasteful of their energy, however, are so because they haven't thought enough about saving it, because they aren't motionminded.

You, in your home, can make use of motionmindedness. Watch the different people in the family. Maybe some of them have it. Maybe you have it yourself.

The person who is motionminded does things in patterns. Each time she repeats a job her hands move in the same curve, and with the same rhythm. A ballet dancer, a baseball player, in fact any expert is worth watching, because the expert does his job with grace and rhythm and economy of motion.

The motionminded person uses both hands effectively. Suppose she is putting eggs in an egg box. With each hand she picks up two eggs from the basket and places them in the box. The nonmotionminded person will pick up the eggs with one hand and hold them, and then with the other hand transfer them to the box.

The motionminded person does not use *large* hand and arm movements where *smaller* ones will do. She uses *smooth* movements rather than *jerky* ones.

Watch a motionminded person doing some mechanical job such as folding towels. She picks up a towel from the pile with both hands, gives it a shake, lays it down, brings the bottom edge to meet the top, folds the right half over to the left, and lays the folded towel aside. She picks up the next towel, does the same thing and places it on top of the first. The other towels are done in the same way. The hands work together, making the same pattern in the air each time. The worker has figured out a little routine for this simple job, and she can talk and look around as she does it, without disturbing the routine.

Now watch a nonmotionminded person doing the same job. She takes a towel, holds it in the air in front of her, folds it in halves, then in quarters, lays it down. She takes another, lays it on the table, folds it first the short way, then the long way. The third one is done long way first. The movements are jerky. She stops now and then to look around, gets careless about bringing the edges together. You talk to her. She stops her work to listen. She seems never to have given any thought to the question, "How shall I do this job?"

Watch a good tennis player. You will see that he does not make any wild, aimless swings or jerky motions. His feet take the fewest possible steps to get him to the place where the ball is going. The motion of his racket arm is smooth and rounded, not zigzag, and its arc is no greater than it needs to be to hit the ball at the right moment. A poor player rushes hither and yon, overshoots the mark and has to run back, swings his racket wildly and misses the ball, pants, scowls, and gets out of breath.

Motion study is helped by visualizing, that is, seeing in advance the whole process of which the motion is a part. The tennis player visualizes the path of the ball and takes steps to get to it. You may not become a Maureen Connolly, but maybe you can train yourself to see the whole of a process as it is done and as it might be done. This requires a very small investment which will begin paying large dividends almost at once.

First, train yourself to observe other people at work. Try in the beginning to observe without letting your subject know he is being watched. Knowing it may make him self-conscious. He may speed up to show you how fast he is, or slow down to impress you with his thoroughness. Sometimes a fast pace is deceiving. Try to time him as he works. If you cannot refer to your watch, time him by counting "one-and-two-and," or "one thousand and one, one thousand and two." You may practice counting with a loud-ticking clock until you can count seconds fairly accurately. Then time the worker to see if he takes the same number of seconds each time he repeats the motion. If he does, he is probably motion-minded. If he lacks rhythm or if he uses fast, erratic motions instead of slower, steadier ones, he probably isn't. Of course it may be that he hasn't learned the job yet, in which case it isn't fair to jump to any conclusions.

Timing *may* show that work done fast is not as well done as work done more slowly. Too fast dusting may leave as much dust on the table tops as on the cloth, and knock over your Royal Doulton porcelain besides. Too fast and too hard scrubbing of painted surfaces, like window sills and bookshelves, may rub off paint and leave streaks. The experienced scrublady uses a leisurely, round-and-round or up-and-down movement that gathers the dirt in the rag and leaves the paint on the surface. (Of course, the most serious result of too fast or too hard work is that it tires the worker prematurely without any proportionate gain in work done.)

On the other hand, in some cases fast work is better than slow. The experienced dressmaker turning up a hem works quickly, taking in a sizable length of hem with each movement. The expert knitter is fast and deft, whereas the beginner is slow and her stitches are alternately loose and tight.

Watch a poor ironer trying to iron a shirt. She may make a lot of fast, jerky motions, running the iron quickly over the collar many times and each time putting new wrinkles into it, hurrying to get the sleeve done before the front gets dry, rushing for a damp cloth to wet the cuffs which weren't properly sprinkled, pressing hard with the iron at one time, and at another sliding it lightly over the cloth again and again without getting the wrinkles out.

Then watch an expert. She lays each part out and irons it with the fewest possible strokes. Her movements are slower, yet she gets the shirt ironed faster and better. The pressure of the iron is even, she goes over each part only once or twice, she knows which part she is going to do first and which next. She folds the shirt automatically with the ease of habit.

If you attached a small electric light to the hand of each worker, and photographed the pattern it made, you would realize how many motions are saved by the expert method.

The established habit is often good motion study, chiefly because it is not necessary to take time out to think of the next step, and because the job is done in the same way each time, and therefore smoothly. Tension and uncertainty are eliminated.

The mere fact that a job is done by habit, however, is not necessarily a good sign. Maybe the habit is a bad one. In one family, for example, the wife wondered why it was that she could wash the dinner dishes usually in twenty minutes, whereas it took her husband three times as long, and each did the job quite by habit. She took note of the differences in method.

It was her practice to put the silver into the dishpan to soak while she did the glasses, and then to put the pile of plates in to soak while she washed them one at a time. Her husband didn't soak anything. He picked up one object at a time from the table, washed it with slow careful strokes of the dish-mop, held it up to the light to look at it, let the water drip off, rinsed it, let the water drip off again, and put it in the draining rack.

The wife washed each dish with a sponge, running her hand over the surface to find out by touch if it was clean. She then placed it quickly in the rinse water and went on to the next plate. After a while she lifted a stack of plates all together from the rinse pan and placed them in the drainer. She didn't hold them up for the water to drip off. Why do that when they would drip in the drainer anyhow? The dishes got just as clean by her method, though it was less painstaking; cleaner in fact because the water stayed hot.

The husband had rhythm and method. He worked by habit But his pace was too slow.

To go back to an activity mentioned in a previous chapter: watch someone making a bed who has never developed a pattern for doing this task. She probably stands at the foot, lays the bottom sheet on, and then runs all around the bed tucking it in. Then she goes back to put on the second sheet, tucking that in. Then she lays the blanket on, and she has to pull out the top sheet to fold it over the blanket. She may get too much of the blanket hanging over on one side and have to pull it up. Or there may be too much or too little tucked in at the bottom. She walks all around the bed again tucking in the blanket. Or she may kneel on the bed and lean across it to tuck the blanket in, if the bed can't be moved out from the wall.

Compare this quite common haphazard method with the one developed at the University of Vermont Agricultural Experiment Station.* Several women were observed as they made beds. One of them walked as much as 262 feet in making one bed. Another walked 188 feet. Diagrams of their paths show yards and yards of backtracking. Though it isn't hard work to walk back and forth, the workers felt annoyed at the tediousness of the job.

A method was worked out in which the whole bed could be made in only one trip around. This is how it was done.

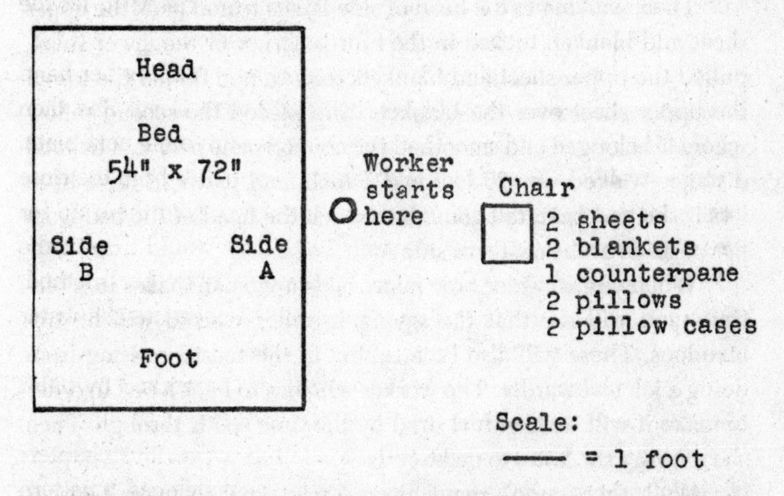

The worker stood at the center of side A. On a chair beside her were 2 sheets, 2 blankets, 1 counterpane, 2 pillows and 2 pillow cases. She took the first sheet, and unfolded it on the bed. Stepping to the head of side A, she tucked the sheet in at the head

* Adapted from Marianne Muse, *Saving Time and Steps in Bedmaking*, Agricultural Experiment Station, University of Vermont and State Agricultural College, Burlington, Vermont, March 1949, Bulletin 551.

and side, and mitered the corner. Stepping back to the center of side A, she got the upper sheet and unfolded it, and did the same with the two blankets, folding the upper sheet back over the top of the blankets. She tossed the counterpane over the bed. She got the two pillows, pulled the case on one, laid it on the A side of the head of the bed, and turned the counterpane over it. She pulled the case on the other, laying it on top of the first.

Then she moved to the foot of side A, tossed back upper sheet and blankets, tucked and mitered the bottom sheet, then tucked and mitered the upper sheet and blankets all together, and pulled the counterpane into place. The next step was to move to the foot of the side B and arrange the sheets, blankets and counterpane at that corner.

Then, walking to the head of side B, she tossed back the upper sheet and blanket, tucked in the fourth corner of the lower sheet, pulled the upper sheet and blankets smooth and folded the top of the upper sheet over the blankets. She placed the second pillow where it belonged and smoothed the counterpane over it. The total distance walked was 23 feet and 1 inch, and it would have been less if she had been tall enough to reach the head of the bed from her position at the center of side A.

When you consider how many beds a woman makes in a lifetime, you will see that the saving in miles walked will be tremendous. There will also be a saving in the tension arising from doing a job awkwardly. The worker who has to fight a bed in order to make it will indeed feel tired by the time she is through. Then she may say she hates to make beds.

Well, there aren't many people who *love* to make beds or would choose it for their life work. Perhaps a bride with her brand-new percale sheets and her fluffy satin-bound blankets, or a young mother lovingly caressing her baby's crib, may linger over her bedmaking. But most of us regard it as a routine chore of minor interest, and manage to get it done in a routine manner with a minimum of tension, so as to proceed to the next job.

Of course if the next job is just as dull or even duller, the worker may slow down from lack of incentive.

Watch ten-year-old Johnny as he cleans up his room on a Saturday morning. He dawdles. He picks up a shoe here, a model airplane there. He stands with a pile of comics in his hands and complains, "I don't know where to put these." His bed is rumpled, his rug is crooked, his desk is piled high with junk of all kinds. He hates the job. Maybe he thinks that if he does it poorly enough, Mother will come in and take over. Maybe he feels that there is no reason for hurrying because when he is done he will just have to sit down and do his homework.

But suppose that instead of doing homework he is going with his uncle to a baseball game—*if* he gets the room cleaned up. What a difference! In ten minutes the desk is clear, the rug is straight, the pajamas are picked up off the floor, the dirty socks are in the laundry hamper. Motion study!

On the other hand, watch Johnny doing a job he likes, the job itself being its own reward—making a model airplane, for instance. He is the picture of concentration. Surely and unhesitatingly he uses the sandpaper, the file, the glue, the jacknife and the paint brush. He is quite efficient. His finger motions are skillful and quick, though if you ask him to set the table he becomes all thumbs and can't lay the silver straight.

Watch your teen-age daughter some time when you have asked her to run the vacuum cleaner in the living room. She's been leaning on the piano reading a magazine. Suddenly she hears your step in the hall. Back and forth the cleaner goes, with a lot of noise, bumping into chairs. She grabs a pile of papers and dumps them in the waste basket. Great activity, but not much in the way of results, chiefly because there was no real incentive to good work. But if she's cleaning up in preparation for a visit from some of her teen-age friends, she may really get busy and do a job. And a job is done most effectively when there is some real need and desire on the part of the worker to get it done.

Remember, however, that it is poor motion study to be a perfectionist—that is, the sort of person who scrapes the dirt out from between the tiles in the bathroom floor with a hairpin, or who irons everything, even the baby's diapers. Do nothing better than it needs to be done.

As we said before, each job has three parts. Industry calls these *get ready, do* and *clean up.*

For instance, in ironing, *get ready* means dampening the clothes, setting up the ironing board, plugging in the iron, getting the table and other furniture arranged conveniently. *Do,* of course, is the ironing process itself. *Clean up* means putting the ironed clothes and equipment away.

In baking a cake, *get ready* means getting out the utensils and ingredients and preparing the oven. *Do* is mixing the batter, pouring it into the pans, putting them in the oven. *Clean up* is putting away the flour, sugar, butter and all the other things, washing the pans and dishes and storing them.

In painting a bookcase, *get ready* means scraping or cleaning the surface, mixing paint, getting out brushes, spreading newspaper. *Do* is the actual painting. *Clean up* means taking paint spots off your hands, putting away the paint, washing and storing brushes, removing newspapers.

In making a dress, *get ready* means clearing a table to lay the material and patterns on, getting out the sewing machine, thread, scissors and other tools, and cutting out the dress. The *do* is a long process involving basting, fitting, sewing, finishing, pressing. *Clean up* means picking up scraps, threads and pins, putting away the machine and other tools, and sweeping the floor.

Usually the *do* is the interesting part of the job, or at any rate the part that accomplishes something, so in planning our time we are apt to forget to allow for the *get ready* and the *clean up.*

Actually the *get ready* and the *clean up* often take more time and energy than the *do.* Certainly they are often more irksome. Perhaps that's why we are apt to skip over them in thinking about the job. They are well worth thinking about, however.

To set up the ironing equipment and wait for the iron to get hot and then put the equipment away again takes about five minutes. To iron a blouse takes about eight minutes. If you set up and put away each time you iron a blouse, that means thirteen minutes for each blouse. If you set up the equipment to iron ten blouses, that means 85 minutes, or only 8.5 minutes per blouse instead of 13. This is a saving of 4.5 minutes per blouse, to say nothing of the energy used up in handling the equipment.

It is easy to see that it is better to set aside a regular time for ironing and get it all done, than to iron a blouse every time you need one.

To get ready for baking and to clean up afterward take about fifteen minutes. Mixing the batter for a cake takes another fifteen minutes, and then you have to wait around for thirty to forty-five minutes while the cake bakes. You may do something else in the meantime but you had better have the cake in mind. This means you can't concentrate very well on what you are doing while the cake is baking. Even if you use a timer you can't go very far away. Obviously it makes sense to bake or cook several things at once while you are at it. You save not only time but also the cost of heating the oven all over again.

To paint a bookcase takes half an hour. But the *get ready* and *clean up* take another half hour, or even more, and cleaning paint brushes is such a bothersome task that many people skip it and let good brushes get stiff with paint.

Obviously, if you have any idea of doing any more painting it would be well to plan to do it all at about the same time.

This, however, is not always possible. Sometimes you want to whip up one cake or paint one little bookcase or iron one blouse or even one handkerchief. If the *get ready* and *clean up* are made quicker and easier, you will feel less resistance to doing these little jobs as they become necessary. You can make them easier by rearranging your work quarters.

You may be able to have a mix center in your kitchen, with everything you need to make a cake within arm's reach, with bowls and pans on handy shelves, spoons and measuring cups on racks above the counter, sugar and flour in bins close by, so that you don't need to climb on a stool for a bowl, or stoop to get a pan out of a pot closet, or lift a heavy flour can off a shelf.

If your electric mixer is standing ready for use on the counter, you will be able to use it at a moment's notice to make your work easier. But if it is dismantled and stored in a closet, it may be more trouble than it's worth to get it out and assemble it.

If the vacuum cleaner is easy to get at, with its cord and hose attached and its bag of tools on a hook near by, you will use it often for small jobs, but if it is stuck away in a box somewhere, you will probably only use it once a week for the main cleaning, and pick up a broom the rest of the time.

If you have a sewing room where the sewing machine can be left ready for use and the ironing board can remain set up, you are really lucky. But if there is no room for this, you can at least store the iron, the cord, the board and a pincushion with needles and thread within a few steps of each other. Then they can be gotten ready to use with the fewest possible motions.

And be sure that things are always returned after use. Good maintenance pays off—a place for everything and everything in its place. Tools should be put back where they came from, and in good condition so that you don't have to stop to look for them or fix them when you need them in a hurry.

Clothes should be mended before being put away.

If the sugar or flour can is empty, fill it before putting the lid back on, or note on your shopping list that more must be bought.

If the can of furniture polish is empty, or the dusters are all dirty, or the vacuum cleaner bag has not been emptied, the work will be delayed because the *get ready* will include something that should have been part of the *clean up* the last time the job was done.

If your schedules are not kept up to date, furs may not be taken out of storage when you want them, woolens may not be taken out of mothballs in time, summer clothes may not be laundered and ready to wear when the hot weather comes. There may be no provision for lunch money, birthday gifts, Christmas cards.

On your desk there should be a check list for purchasing supplies, including everything you use in your home, so that you can run your eye down it quickly before you go shopping. There should also be a calendar or some other reminder system to tell you in advance of jobs to be done or purchases to be made.

Some jobs take a long time on the *get ready,* others on the *clean up.* Keeping this in mind, you can plan your work intelligently.

If you are planning a picnic, for instance, you may prepare potato salad, fried chicken, chocolate cake, sandwiches—food that takes a long time to fix but for which there is almost no *clean up.*

If the painters are coming, you quickly get bric-a-brac put away and closets emptied, but plan for a good long *clean up.*

The *get ready* or the *clean up* may be cut down by a change of method. Processed food, cake mixes, frozen and ready-cooked food make preparation easy and *clean up* quick.

For the laundry, detergents may be used that make soaking unnecessary.

Clothes or furniture may be bought that require little care.

Nylon or fiberglass curtains are easy to wash, dry quickly, and need no ironing.

The *get ready* may be moved to a more convenient hour. For instance, a casserole meal may be prepared in the morning to be served at night. Sandwiches or soups or pies or roast fowl may be made in quantity and kept in the deep freeze. The deep freeze, in fact, is one of this century's greatest gifts to modern housekeepers, if they have room for one, and money to buy it with.

Clothing for the morning may be laid out at night. Garments coming back from the cleaner or new clothes coming from the store should be examined before being put away, to be sure they are ready to wear.

Sometimes a job can't be finished all at one time. Then convenient storage places for unfinished work must be devised—a drawer for unironed clothes, a box for unsorted letters, a basket for things to be mended.

Gadgets are fun and are often useful. Make sure the ones you have are efficient and, if they are, that you are using them. If not, get rid of them. Manufacturers are constantly making new ones. They have to, to stay in business, but you don't have to buy them.

Melon ball cutters, potato shredders, fancy patty shell makers, trick ice crushers, cute cooky cutters have a way of piling up in the kitchen drawer while you go on cutting melons with a paring knife and cookies with the top of the baking powder can.

A pressure cooker is a wonderful thing. Read the instructions and use a timer. If it helps you get your dinner ready sooner and if you like the flavor of the food that comes out of it, it's worth its keep, but if not, don't give it house room. You want things around that will help you, not clutter up the place.

This applies to people, too. If you ask for help, know what you want the helpers to do before calling them in. Be an executive, with guests as well as with members of the family. People like to be told what you want. Otherwise they will either take over the work themselves and do it in a way you don't want, or they will just lean against the wall and talk to you while *you* work.

Try to give the helpers jobs they will like. Many people like the *do*, but don't like the *get ready* or *clean up*. Men often like to cook but not to wash up. Or they may like to shop but not to make lists or put things away. Let them do the things they prefer while you handle the rest of the cycle.

It pays to encourage young Johnny to come into the kitchen by giving him an important job to do like turning the pancakes or stirring the jam, instead of always making him dry the silver or set the table. A chef's cap and apron and some warm praise have been known to help. Don't forget to announce to the family, "Johnny made these muffins. Try them, they're delicious."

Sometimes you need help in heavy work, such as moving furniture or taking down draperies or putting up storm windows. You must plan to do the work when the strong males of the family are at liberty. Arrange your *get ready* accordingly. Have the windows washed so you don't have to stop to do it while Father waits around doing nothing, or goes off to start some other job.

Sometimes your helpers turn out to be more motionminded than you are yourself. Do not scorn to listen to their ideas. If Johnny complains while drying the silver that the knife rack is in a very inconvenient place, explain to him that you put it there so that the knives would be handy when you want to use one, even though the rack was not so handy for putting away. He may suggest a better place for both purposes. A fresh point of view often results in fresh ideas.

Men often have good ideas about housework chiefly because they don't like it much. The engineers sometimes say that they are careful to observe the laziest person in the plant. He is the one who thinks up short cuts. Men are apt to have good ideas about using wheels, inclined planes, pivoting storage walls, pulleys, improved storage places, better lighting.

Being motionminded is a matter of imagination. Once you free your imagination by questioning your old ways of doing things, it goes ahead and produces new ideas by the score. Don't be afraid to let it loose.

Chapter 4

Charts

So far we've been talking about general principles of work simplification. This chapter is going to be somewhat technical. If you're going in for household engineering in a big way, you may want to concentrate on it. If not, you may skim through it so you'll know the meaning of the technical terms used, and go on to the next. Or you may want to skip it entirely and come back to it later, when you've had time to think about specific changes to be made in your own home.

Previously we discussed what jobs should be done, who should do them, where and when they should be done. This chapter will try to answer the question, "*How* should this job be done?"

The engineer in the factory may think he knows of a better way to can tomatoes. But he can't just go to the owner and say, "Look here, I've got a hunch that if you buy a lot of new equipment and rebuild your factory you'll be able to cut down on time and increase your production."

That would be most inaccurate and unscientific. He has to reduce his proposals to scientific statements. He has to have records of how the job is done, so that he can show where it should be changed, and exactly what will be gained by the change. He has many ways to do this. One way is the process chart.

In the process chart the engineer gives a description of every step used in doing the job. Then he studies the chart. He questions each step, asking whether it is necessary, whether it can be combined with other steps, whether the work place is well arranged, whether the tools are right, and so on. Then he makes another process chart showing the revised method of doing the job.

You can do this, too. Make process charts of some of your household tasks and see what a clear picture you get of what you are doing and how you might improve.

First, turn to your ever-useful notebook and make a new division, entitled, "Process charts."

Now choose some simple chore that you do quite frequently. It should be a simple task to start with, and it should be one you do often, because you are familiar with it and do it according to a fixed routine, which makes it easy to chart, and because the saving you make will be a help to you at once.

Let us assume you are going to chart the job of making coffee. At the head of the page put the name of the job, in the form of a job description, as follows:

Making breakfast coffee for two, present method

This is important because it sets limits to the job. You know it doesn't mean after-dinner coffee for six.

Have someone work with you, if possible, to watch and make notes of what you do. But if you can't get a helper you can do it alone, only of course it will take longer, since you have to stop and write a description of your motions.

The person who is making notes must observe where you start the job and where you end. She must then list all your motions, how far you walk in any direction and where you go. She may make a note of the time taken.

Now here is a little device that engineers have found useful. When jobs are broken down into their basic parts, they are found to consist of certain main divisions. The engineers simplify their charts by describing work in terms of these divisions, and they use symbols for them—a kind of shorthand.

Here are the five main divisions and their symbols:

○ **Operations—doing something to the materials.**

➪ **Transportations—carrying materials, or moving from place to place.**

□ **Inspections—examining the work or reading instructions.**

D **Delays—time wasted while the worker waits for something to happen.**

▽ **Storages—putting materials or finished products away.**

Here are some examples of these in a household:

OPERATIONS

Mixing cake
Peeling vegetables
Washing dishes
Adding salt to pan of food
Ironing clothes

TRANSPORTATIONS

Moving by tea cart
Moving by pulling rope
Moving by carrying
Moving by pulling
Moving by pushing
Walking from one place to another

INSPECTIONS

Counting sheets in laundry sent or returned
Weighing purchases
Checking groceries with cash register slip
Measuring ingredients for recipe
Checking clothes for repairs while ironing

Reading instructions on package of cereal
Looking at food during cooking process

DELAYS

Waiting for water to boil
Discovering supply of floor polish exhausted
" pieces of dress pattern missing
" broken knife
Waiting for husband or child when late

STORAGES

Putting vegetables in wire bin
Putting food in refrigerator
Putting supplies in cupboards or closets
Putting linens on shelves

Now to get back to the process chart. Make three columns. The first will be labeled "What is done," the second will be for symbols, the third for distance traveled, in linear feet or steps. Make a small drawing of your workroom and tell where the job begins and where it ends.

You must decide on the boundaries of the job. They should include the *get ready* and the *clean up*. You must also decide what method you will use, if there is a choice. There are several ways of making coffee (percolator, vacuum maker, drip pot, etc.). Let us say you are using a drip pot with a pan to heat water. You must get the utensils, the water, the coffee, and the measuring tools.

Your chart may read something like this:

JOB: MAKING BREAKFAST COFFEE FOR TWO, PRESENT METHOD

(Chart begins at kitchen door, ends at table)

WHAT IS DONE	SYMBOL	STEPS
1. To food cupboard	⇨	5
2. Get coffee	○	
3. To range. Leave coffee there	⇨	5
4. To dish closet	⇨	4
5. Get measuring cup and spoon	○	
6. To pan cupboard	⇨	2
7. Get coffee pot	○	
8. To range with coffee pot, cup and spoon	⇨	4
9. Open can of coffee	○	
10. Take lid off coffee pot	○	
11. Measure one spoon of coffee	□	
12. Place in coffee basket	○	
13. Measure second spoon of coffee	□	
14. Place in coffee basket	○	
15. Measure third spoon of coffee	□	
16. Place in coffee basket	○	
17. Measure fourth spoon of coffee	□	
18. Place in coffee basket	○	
19. Replace lid on coffee can	○	
20. To pan cupboard	⇨	4
21. Get saucepan	○	
22. To sink	⇨	4

WHAT IS DONE	SYMBOL	STEPS
23. Reach for cup	○	
24. Turn on water	○	
25. Measure one cup of water	□	
26. Pour into saucepan	○	
27. Measure second cup of water	□	
28. Pour into saucepan	○	
29. Measure third cup of water	□	
30. Pour into saucepan	○	
31. Measure fourth cup of water	□	
32. Pour into saucepan	○	
33. To range	⇨	2
34. Put saucepan on burner	○	
35. Light burner	○	
36. To sink	⇨	2
37. Rinse spoon	○	
38. Dry spoon and cup	○	
39. To dish closet	⇨	4
40. Put away spoon and cup	▽	
41. Wait for water to boil	D	
42. To range	⇨	4
43. Pour water into coffee pot	○	
44. To food cupboard	⇨	5
45. Put away coffee	▽	
46. To range	⇨	5
47. Take coffee pot to table	⇨	4

A count will show that there were 14 transportations, 22 operations, 8 inspections, 2 storages and 1 delay and you took 54 steps.

Look at the chart again and see if you can eliminate any motions. Can you combine any? Can you change the sequence of operations? Can you simplify? You certainly can.

First, store the saucepan on a shelf near the sink. Then you can go right to the sink, fill the pan, and put the water to boil before measuring the coffee, thus cutting out some delay. Use hot water instead of cold, cutting out more delay, if this water is satisfactory to drink. You can mark the saucepan so that you need only run the water into the pan, thus eliminating the measuring cup. Use both hands. Reach for the pan with one hand and turn on the water with the other. Put the pan on the stove with one hand and light the gas with the other.

Now reach for the coffee pot and the coffee, which have been moved to a shelf near the stove. Mark the coffee basket so you can pour the required amount of coffee in without a measuring spoon. Or get a measure that holds all you need and put all the coffee in at once. Now do the job again. Here is your new chart:

JOB: MAKING BREAKFAST COFFEE FOR TWO, IMPROVED METHOD

(Chart begins at kitchen door, ends at table)

WHAT IS DONE	SYMBOL	STEPS
1. To sink	⇨	3
2. Get saucepan and turn on water	○	
3. Run water to line in pan	□	
4. To range	⇨	2
5. Put pan on burner and light gas	○	
6. Get coffee and coffee pot	○	
7. Open can and take off lid of pot	○	
8. Pour coffee into basket to measuring line	□	
9. Wait for water to boil	D	
10. Pour water into pot	○	
11. Put lid on coffee can	○	
12. Put away coffee	▽	
13. Take coffee pot to table	⇨	4

You can now see that you have reduced the process to 3 transportations, 6 operations, 2 inspections, 1 storage and 1 delay (during which you could, of course, be getting out the cups and the cream and sugar), and you took only 9 steps instead of 54. A worthwhile saving.

Of course, it is obvious that when you make your improved chart, the starting point and the finishing point should be the same as in the chart for the old method. It wouldn't be fair to start from the living room in the old method and from the kitchen door in the new one, and then say, "Look how many steps we saved!"

This applies to the method, too. It would not make sense to use ground coffee with a drip pot in one case, and instant coffee in another, unless the use of instant coffee is part of the new process and you are setting out to prove that time and energy can be saved by using instant instead of regular coffee.

There is another kind of chart that you can make, which will dramatize even more the amount of walking around that you do in your home. This is the flow chart. A combination of the flow and process charts really gives you a picture of what goes on.

To make the flow chart, first make a scale drawing of your kitchen. Use squared paper, and let one square equal one foot on your kitchen floor. Put in the furniture and apparatus, also to scale.

Take the process chart which you have made. Suppose the process chart says you started at the kitchen door and walked to the pot cupboard. Draw a line on the chart from door to cupboard. Then if you went to the sink, draw a line from cupboard to sink. Draw a line for each trip you made until you get to the end of the process. Now you can measure the number of feet you traveled. If you went back and forth over the same ground many times, the chart is apt to look something like a kindergarten child's scrawl, and you may have difficulty in measuring.

Another method is to make a string chart. Mount the chart on cardboard, to give it firmness, and stick pins or brass paper fasteners into the chart at all the points where the worker stops or turns. Then you wind string, which you have previously measured, around the pins or fasteners.

Suppose you start with five feet of string, and have one foot left after you are through winding. You have used up four feet, and you can figure out how many feet of travel they represent.

For a permanent chart, fasteners are better than pins because they don't come out.

On the next page you will see two string charts. They represent the floor plan of the Heart Kitchen, a model kitchen designed for the American Heart Association, to show how a woman with a

STRING CHARTS—ORIGINAL AND IMPROVED

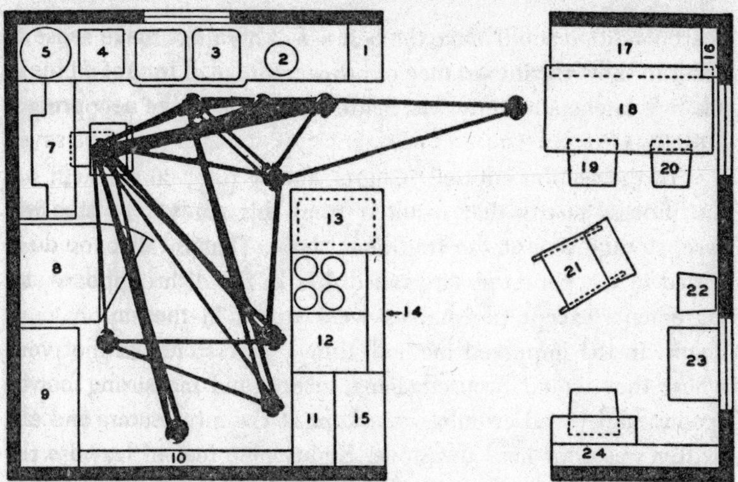

1. Shelves (*Open from both sides*). 2. Garbage Disposal and Paring Center. 3. Double Sink. 4. Washing Machine. 5. Revolving Shelves. 6. Work Chair. 7. Mix Center (*Baking and mixing*). 8. Refrigerator (*Handle of door is next to mix counter*). 9. Storage for Cleaning Tools. 10. Grocery Storage (*Week's supply for family of four.*) 11. Storage for Cooking Utensils. 12. Range and Oven. 13. Work Counter (*Wheeled table underneath*). 14, 15. Storage for Company Dinnerware. 16. Storage Shelf. 17. Dinette Bench Toy and Hobby Storage. 18. Dinette Table. 19, 20. Dinette Chairs. 21. Rocker. 22. Chair. 23. Record Player. 24. Planning Center and Book Shelves.

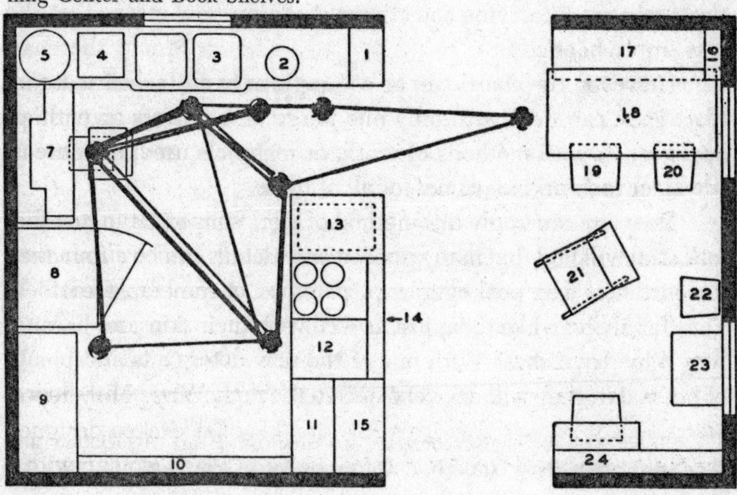

heart condition could make the best use of her time and energy. In order to show the importance of proper storage of foods and utensils in a kitchen, a study was made of the process of preparing a meat loaf.

In the section entitled "Charts" facing page 86 you will see the process charts that resulted from this study.* In the first case, storage was of the traditional type. That is, all pans were stored in the pan cupboard, all dishes in the dish cupboard, all ingredients except perishables were stored in the supply cupboard. In the improved method, things were stored at the point where they would be used. Pans, mixing and measuring bowls, spoons, and bread crumbs were kept at the mix center, and the platter was kept near the stove. Eighty-nine feet of travel were saved. This is shown graphically on the string charts, and in more detail on the process charts. People who use these charts frequently use printed forms like the ones shown. You will see that the different centers and pieces of furniture are numbered on the floor plan, and these numbers appear on the process chart for easy identification. These charts are concerned only with savings in operations and transportations (the shaded arrow indicates that the worker was carrying something. A plain arrow means that she was empty-handed).

However, the charts can be as simple or as all-inclusive as you like. They can deal with only one phase of a process or with all angles of it; with methods of work, or materials used, or route of travel, or tools and machines, or all of these.

Now you can apply this method of work simplification to other jobs. You will find that many unnecessary details can be *eliminated.* For instance, why peel eggplants, potatoes, cucumbers, tomatoes? Your family may like them just as well with their skins on.

Why dry dishes? With one of the new detergents and plenty of hot water, they will dry very well in the rack. Why polish floors?

* Flow process charts courtesy of American Heart Association and Teachers College, New York, N.Y. Drawn by Jane Callaghan.

Use a no-rubbing floor wax and simply spread it on.

You can eliminate details by changing the place of work. If you squeeze oranges at the sink, you make the mopping up of spilled juice unnecessary. Fill jars with fruit or jam over the sink and save wiping. Pour sugar or flour into containers over the drainboard or on a newspaper.

Combine details wherever possible. Clothes can be taken from the line and folded ready for use in one operation. Mending can be done as you iron. Store your jewelry, stockings and other accessories with the clothes with which you wear them—evening things together, sports clothes, and so on.

Foods can be stored in the quantity used. Canned goods can be put up in pints for a small family, with a few quarts for a company meal. Frozen food can be put up in containers of any size, even down to individual portions. It can also be assembled in complete meals, with menus for four, six or even ten persons. Then all the housewife need do is take one package from the freezer and serve.

You can improve by changing the *sequence* of jobs. Measure dry ingredients first, then wet, and use only one set of measuring tools instead of two.

Changing the sequence often makes the job easier. For instance, red beets can be peeled and sliced easily after cooking. Large squash can be cut up more easily *after* steaming or baking than before. Pots and pans can be scoured more easily *after* washing in the automatic dishwasher.

Do your cleaning in the right sequence by going all around the room once instead of running back and forth across it. Start upstairs and work your way down. Start at the top of a room and work down, dusting the walls, then the furniture, then the floor.

At some times a job can be done in a leisurely way. At other times pressure not only makes the job unpleasant, but causes unexpected delays. See that clothes and books are laid out in the evening when there is plenty of time, so they won't have to be looked for in the morning rush hour. Do your Christmas shopping early.

Simplify operations by changing your equipment or tools, when it seems to be worth while. But here a warning is needed. Modern advertising has drummed it into our heads that the best labor-saving device is a new piece of machinery. The new products are increasingly marvelous and beautiful, but they may not always be the answer. For example, the housewife may think she needs a brand new mixer, whereas the amount of mixing she does may not warrant such an expense, and all she really needs is a rearrangement of her present tools into an efficient mix center. She may hate to iron and wish for an electric ironer. But for the amount of ironing she does, all that is really needed may be an ironing board of the proper height so she won't get that backache.

Instead of rushing out to buy new large equipment, see that your small tools are of good design, that you have as many simple mechanical aids as possible, such as shelves and tables of the right height, and a comfortable work chair, and that you improve the "how" by using your motionmindedness.

Think of the different jobs you do, and the demands they make, and think of yourself in relation to them. Decide how much work it is worth while to cut out.

Ask yourself these questions:

1. *Do I like activity?* If you do, then you won't want to cut it all out. You may decide you'd rather wash a few clothes in a tub by hand, because you don't mind the exertion and it's less trouble than getting the machine out.

If you don't like exertion, or if you *ought* to cut out as much as possible, then be sure you are getting every possible aid. Have every advantage of machinery and good design that you can afford. In the Heart Kitchen, mentioned above, all the principles of scientific management were used to save walking, stooping, reaching, lifting and other unnecessary motions. You don't have to have a heart condition to enjoy some of these advantages.

Charts

On the following pages you will see examples of the charts that have been mentioned in the text. The flow process charts show the original and improved methods of making a meat loaf in the Heart Kitchen, illustrated also by the string charts on page 83.

The micromotion transfer sheet (original method) was made as the engineer watched a film showing eggs being transferred from a box to a tray. The simo chart shows the same process spread out so that you can really see how much time was taken for each motion.

The improved method illustrates graphically the saving made when both hands worked together.

FLOW PROCESS CHART

NO. 1

TEACHERS COLLEGE — COLUMBIA UNIVERSITY — DEPARTMENT OF HOME ECONOMICS

SUBJECT CHARTED PREPARATION OF MEAT LOAF TRADITIONAL KITCHEN STORAGE

SUMMARY

	PRESENT NO.	PRESENT TIME	PROPOSED NO.	PROPOSED TIME	DIFFERENCE NO.	DIFFERENCE TIME
○ OPERATIONS	25					
⇨ TRANSPORTATIONS	32					
□ INSPECTIONS						
D DELAYS						
▽ STORAGES						
DISTANCE TRAVELLED	196 FT.		FT.		FT.	

PRESENT [X] OR PROPOSED [ ] METHOD

TYPE OF CHART [X] MAN OR [ ] MATERIAL

CHART BEGINS AT RANGE

CHART ENDS AT CLEANING CLOSET

CHARTED BY O.M.THOMAS DATE 4/21/54

DESCRIPTION OF EVENT	Equipment location on plan	OPERATION / TRANSPORT / INSPECTION / DELAY / STORAGE	DISTANCE IN FEET	QUANTITY	TIME	ANALYSIS WHY? WHAT? WHERE? WHEN? WHO? HOW?	NOTES	ACTION: ELIMINATE / CHNGE: COMBINE, SEQUE., PLACE, PERSON / IMPROVE
1. Light oven	12	○⇨□D▽						
2. To cleaning closet	9	○⇨□D▽	6					
3. Get apron		○⇨□D▽						
4. To pan cupboard	11	○⇨□D▽	6					
5. Get loaf pan		○⇨□D▽						
6. To mixing center	7	○⇨□D▽	$10\frac{1}{2}$					
7. Leave loaf pan		○⇨□D▽						
8. To dish cupboard	1	○⇨□D▽	$6\frac{1}{2}$					
9. Get bowl and measuring cup		○⇨□D▽						
10. To mixing center	7	○⇨□D▽	$6\frac{1}{2}$					
11. Get mixing spoon		○⇨□D▽						
12. To supply cupboard	10	○⇨□D▽	9					
13. Get bread crumbs		○⇨□D▽						
14. To mixing center	7	○⇨□D▽	9					
15. Get meat eggs, fat, milk and catsup from refrig.	8	○⇨□D▽						
16. Measure ingredients		○⇨□D▽						
17. Break eggs		○⇨□D▽						
18. Mix loaf		○⇨□D▽						
19. Grease loaf pan		○⇨□D▽						
20. Put loaf into pan		○⇨□D▽						
21. Take loaf to oven	12	○⇨□D▽	8					
TIME INTERVAL		○⇨□D▽						
22. To mix center	7	○⇨□D▽	8					
23. To garbage can	2	○⇨□D▽	6					
24. Discard egg shells and paper		○⇨□D▽						
25. To mix center	7	○⇨□D▽	6					
26. Ingredients to refrigerator	8	○⇨□D▽						
27. To supply cupboard	10	○⇨□D▽	9					

28. Leave bread crumbs		
29. To mixing center	7	9
30. Get used utensils and tools		
31. To sink	3	3½
32. Wash utensils and tools		
33. Bowl & cup to dish cupboard	1	4
34. To sink	3	4
35. Spoon to mix center	7	3½
36. To dish cupboard	1	4
37. Get platter		
38. Take platter to range	13	3
39. To mixing center	7	6
40. Get spatula		
41. To range	12	8
42. Take loaf from oven		
43. Take loaf to serving center	13	3
44. Place loaf on platter		
45. Take utensils to sink	3	4
46. Put pan to soak		
47. To serving center	13	4
48. Put platter on serving cart		
49. Serving cart with rest of meal to dining area	18	8
TIME INTERVAL		
50. Serving cart to sink	3	10
51. Wash dishes		
52. Platter to dish cupboard	1	4
53. Return to sink	3	4
54. Loaf pan to pan cupboard	11	7
55. To sink	3	7
56. Spatula to mix center	7	3½
57. Apron to cleaning closet	9	6

FLOW PROCESS CHART

NO. 2

TEACHERS COLLEGE — COLUMBIA UNIVERSITY — DEPARTMENT OF HOME ECONOMICS

SUBJECT CHARTED PREPARATION OF MEAT LOAF FUNCTIONAL KITCHEN STORAGE

SUMMARY

	PRESENT NO.	PRESENT TIME	PROPOSED NO.	PROPOSED TIME	DIFFERENCE NO.	DIFFERENCE TIME
○ OPERATIONS	25		21		4	
⇨ TRANSPORTATIONS	32		18		14	
□ INSPECTIONS						
D DELAYS						
▽ STORAGES						
DISTANCE TRAVELLED	196 FT.		107 FT.		89 FT. or 45.4% saved	

PRESENT ☐ OR PROPOSED ☒ METHOD

TYPE OF CHART ☒ MAN OR ☐ MATERIAL

CHART BEGINS AT RANGE

CHART ENDS AT CLEANING CLOSET

CHARTED BY O.M.THOMAS DATE 4/24/54

DESCRIPTION OF EVENT	Equipment location on plan	Symbol	DISTANCE IN FEET	QUANTITY	TIME	ANALYSIS WHY? (WHAT? WHERE? WHEN? WHO? HOW?)	NOTES	ACTION (ELIMINATE, COMBINE, CHNGE: SEQUE., PLACE, PERSON)
1. Light oven	12	Operation						
2. Go to cleaning closet	9	Transport	6					
3. Get apron		Operation						
4. To mixing center	7	Transport	6					
5. Get loaf pan, mixing bowl, measuring cup, spoon, crumbs		Operation						
6. Get refrigerated supplies	8	Operation						
7. Measure ingredients		Operation						
8. Break eggs		Operation						
9. Mix loaf		Operation						
10. Grease loaf pan		Operation						
11. Put loaf into pan		Operation						
12. Take loaf to oven	12	Transport (filled)	8					
TIME INTERVAL								
13. Return to mix center	7	Transport	8					
14. To garbage can	2	Transport (filled)	6					
15. Discard egg shells and wrapping paper		Operation						
16. Return to mix center	7	Transport	6					
17. Return ingredients to refrigerator		Operation						
18. Return bread crumbs to supply shelf		Operation						
19. Get used utensils and tools		Operation						
20. To sink	3	Transport (filled)	3½					
21. Wash utensils and tools		Operation						
22. Return utensils and tools to mix center	7	Transport (filled)	3½					
TIME INTERVAL								
23. To range center	12	Transport	8					

Step		Symbols	
24. Get platter		○ ⇨ □ D ▽	
25. Get spatula		○ ⇨ □ D ▽	
26. Remove loaf with hot pads		○ ⇨ □ D ▽	
27. Plave loaf on platter		○ ⇨ □ D ▽	
28. To serving center	13	○ ➡ □ D ▽	5½
29. Take pan and spatula to sink	3	○ ➡ □ D ▽	2
30. Put pan to soak		○ ⇨ □ D ▽	
31. To serving center	13	○ ⇨ □ D ▽	2
32. Put platter on serving cart		○ ⇨ □ D ▽	
33. Serving cart to dining area	18	○ ➡ □ D ▽	8
TIME INTERVAL		○ ⇨ □ D ▽	
34. Serving cart and dishes to sink	3	○ ➡ □ D ▽	10
35. Wash dishes		○ ⇨ □ D ▽	
36. Return platter to range center 12, and spatula to serving center, 13		○ ➡ □ D ▽	7½
37. To sink	3	○ ⇨ □ D ▽	7½
38. Loaf pan to mixing center	7	○ ➡ □ D ▽	3½
39. Apron to cleaning closet	9	○ ➡ □ D ▽	6

Original Method

Sheet No. 1 of 1

Date Made 6/6/54

MICRO-MOTION TRANSFER SHEET

R. Doe

Film No. 151

Date Filmed May 15, 1954

By Robert E. Doe

Operation Transferring eggs

Operator Jane Doe

Department

Clock Reading No. Frames	Subtracted Time	Therblig Symbol	DESCRIPTION LEFT HAND	Clock Reading No. Frames	Subtracted Time	Therblig Symbol	DESCRIPTION RIGHT HAND
0	16	TE	To egg tray	0	3	H	Hold tray
16	15	G	Grasp tray	3	19	TL	Pick up tray
31	705	H	Hold tray	22	2	RL	Release tray
736	10	RL	Release tray	24	12	TE	To egg box
746	45	TE	To starting position	36	15	G&PP	Grasp and pre-position egg
791	X	D	Wait	51	18	TL	To egg tray
				69	2	P&RL	Position and release egg
				71	19	TE	To egg box
				90	66	G&PP	Grasp and pre-position egg
				156	30	TL	To egg tray
				186	3	P&RL	Position and release egg
				189	13	TE	To egg box
				202	15	G&PP	Grasp and pre-position egg
				217	21	TL	To egg tray
				238	11	P&RL	Position and release egg
				249	13	TE	To egg box
				262	18	G&PP	Grasp and pre-position egg
				280	17	TL	To egg tray
				297	9	P&RL	Position and release egg
				306	9	TE	To egg box
				315	24	G&PP	Grasp and pre-position egg
				339	12	TL	To egg tray
				351	8	P&RL	Position and release egg
				359	13	TE	To egg box
				372	15	G&PP	Grasp and pre-position egg
				387	17	TL	To egg tray
				404	7	P&RL	Position and release egg
				411	13	TE	To egg box
				424	17	G&PP	Grasp and pre-position egg
				441	10	TL	To egg tray
				451	10	P&RL	Position and release egg
				461	16	TE	To egg box
				477	17	G&PP	Grasp and pre-position egg
				494	16	TL	To egg tray
				510	7	P&RL	Position and release egg
				517	10	TE	To egg box
				527	15	G&PP	Grasp and pre-position egg
				542	17	TL	To egg tray
				559	9	P&RL	Position and release egg
				568	11	TE	To egg box
				579	13	G&PP	Grasp and pre-position egg
				592	14	TL	To egg tray
				606	11	P&RL	Position and release egg
				617	9	TE	To egg box
				626	14	G&PP	Grasp and pre-position egg
				640	12	TL	To egg tray
				652	14	P&RL	Position and release egg
				666	13	TE	To egg box
				679	11	G&PP	Grasp and pre-position egg
				690	15	TL	To egg tray
				705	13	P&RL	Position and release egg
				718	27	G	Grasp entire tray
				745	17	TL	Place on counter
				762	10	RL	Release tray
				772	19	TE	To original starting position
				791	X	D	Wait

Original Method

SIMULTANEOUS MOTION CHART

OPERATION Transferring eggs from box to tray **DATE** June 6, 1954

METHOD NOW IN USE X **ANALYST** Robert E. Doe

NEW METHOD BEST CYCLE ______ **IDEAL CYCLE** ______ **TIME UNIT** 1/1000 min.

Left Hand Description	Sym.	Time	Accrued Time
To egg tray	TE	16	16
Grasp tray	G	15	31
Hold tray	H	705	

CLOCK OR METER READING: 0, 20, 40, 60, 80, 100, 120, 140, 160, 180, 200, 220, 240, 260, 280, 300, 320, 340, 360, 380, 400, 420

Accrued Time	Time	Sym.	Right Hand Description
3	3	H	Hold tray
22	19	TL	Pick up tray
24	2	RL	Release tray
36	12	TE	To egg box
51	15	G&PP	Grasp and pre-position egg
69	18	TL	To egg tray
71	2	P&RL	Position and release egg
90	19	TE	To egg box
156	66	G&PP	Grasp and pre-position egg
186	30	TL	To egg tray
189	3	P&RL	Position and release egg
202	13	TE	To egg box
217	15	G&PP	Grasp and pre-position egg
238	21	TL	To egg tray
249	11	P&RL	Position and release egg
262	13	TE	To egg box
280	18	G&PP	Grasp and pre-position egg
297	17	TL	To egg tray
306	9	P&RL	Position and release egg
315	9	TE	To egg box
339	24	G&PP	Grasp and pre-position egg
351	12	TL	To egg tray
359	8	P&RL	Position and release egg
372	13	TE	To egg box
387	15	G&PP	Grasp and pre-position egg
404	17	TL	To egg tray
411	7	P&RL	Position and release egg
	13	TE	To egg box

Left hand

Description	Symbol	Time	Time marks
Release tray	RL	10	736
To original starting position	TE	45	746
			791

Right hand

Time marks	Time	Symbol	Description
424	17	G&PP	Grasp and pre-position egg
441	10	TL	To egg tray
451	10	P&RL	Position and release egg
461	16	TE	To egg box
477	17	G&PP	Grasp and pre-position egg
494	16	TL	To egg tray
510	7	P&RL	Position and release egg
517	10	TE	To egg box
527	15	G&PP	Grasp and pre-position egg
542	17	TL	To egg tray
559	9	P&RL	Position and release egg
568	11	TE	To egg box
579	13	G&PP	Grasp and pre-position egg
592	14	TL	To egg tray
606	11	P&RL	Position and release egg
617	9	TE	To egg box
626	14	G&PP	Grasp and pre-position egg
640	12	TL	To egg tray
652	14	P&RL	Position and release egg
666	13	TE	To egg box
679	11	G&PP	Grasp and pre-position egg
690	15	TL	To egg tray
705	13	P&RL	Position and release egg
718	27	G	Grasp entire tray
745	17	TL	Place on counter
762	10	RL	Release tray
772	19	TE	To original starting position
791			

Time scale: 440, 460, 480, 500, 520, 540, 560, 580, 600, 620, 640, 660, 680, 700, 720, 740, 760, 780, 800

<u>Left hand summary</u>

%	Symbol	Time
8%	TE	61
2%	G	15
89%	H	705
1%	RL	10
100%		

<u>**Right Hand Summary**</u>

Time	Symbol	%
3	H	0.5%
235	TL	30.0%
64	RL	8.0%
170	TE	20.5%
147	G	19.0%
120	PP	15.0%
52	P	7.0%
		100.0%

Improved Method

Sheet No. 1 of
Date Made 6/6/54
By R. Doe

MICRO-MOTION TRANSFER SHEET

Film No. 152
Date Filmed May 15, 1954
By Robert E. Doe

Operation Transferring Eggs
Operator Jane Doe
Department

Clock Reading No. Frames	Subtracted Time	Therblig Symbol	DESCRIPTION **LEFT HAND**	Clock Reading No. Frames	Subtracted Time	Therblig Symbol	DESCRIPTION **RIGHT HAND**
0	21	TE	To egg carton	0	17	TE	To egg carton
21	20	G&PP	Grasp and pre-position egg	17	23	G&PP	Grasp and pre-position egg
41	14	TL	To egg tray	40	16	TL	To egg tray
55	16	P&RL	Position and release egg	56	15	P&RL	Position and release egg
71	14	TE	To egg carton	71	11	TE	To egg carton
85	51	G&PP	Grasp and pre-position egg	82	50	G&PP	Grasp and pre-position egg
136	15	TL	To egg tray	132	19	TL	To egg tray
151	10	P&RL	Position and release egg	151	10	P&RL	Position and release egg
161	20	TE	To egg carton	161	17	TE	To egg carton
181	6	G&PP	Grasp and pre-position egg	178	11	G&PP	Grasp and pre-position egg
187	23	TL	To egg tray	189	21	TL	To egg tray
210	9	P&RL	Position and release egg	210	9	P&RL	Position and release egg
219	12	TE	To egg carton	219	12	TE	To egg carton
231	21	G&PP	Grasp and pre-position egg	231	21	G&PP	Grasp and pre-position egg
252	14	TL	To egg tray	252	14	TL	To egg tray
266	15	P&RL	Position and release egg	266	15	P&RL	Position and release egg
281	14	TE	To egg carton	281	14	TE	To egg carton
295	22	G&PP	Grasp and pre-position egg	295	22	G&PP	Grasp and pre-position egg
317	19	TL	To egg tray	317	19	TL	To egg tray
336	16	P&RL	Position and release egg	336	14	P&RL	Position and release egg
350	17	TE	To egg carton	350	11	TE	To egg carton
367	23	G&PP	Grasp and pre-position egg	361	29	G&PP	Grasp and pre-position egg
390	17	TL	To egg tray	390	17	TL	To egg tray
407	18	P&RL	Position and release egg	407	18	P&RL	Position and release egg
425	20	TE	To starting position	425	20	TE	To starting position
445	X			445	X		

Improved method

SIMULTANEOUS MOTION CHART

OPERATION Transferring eggs from box to tray **DATE** June 6, 1954

METHOD NOW IN USE ______ **ANALYST** Robert E. Doe

NEW METHOD BEST CYCLE X **IDEAL CYCLE** ______ **TIME UNIT** 1/1000 min.

Left Hand

Left Hand Description	Sym.	Time	Accrued Time
To egg carton	TE	21	21
Grasp and pre-position egg	G&PP	20	41
To egg tray	TL	14	55
Position and release egg	P&RL	16	71
To egg carton	TE	14	85
Grasp and pre-position egg	G&PP	51	136
To egg tray	TL	15	151
Position and release egg	P&RL	10	161
To egg carton	TE	20	181
Grasp & pre-position egg	G&PP	6	187
To egg tray	TL	23	210
Position & release egg	P&RL	9	219
To egg carton	TE	12	231
Grasp & pre-position egg	G&PP	21	252
To egg tray	TL	14	266
Position & release egg	P&RL	15	281
To egg carton	TE	14	295
Grasp & Pre-position egg	G&PP	22	317
To egg tray	TL	19	336
Position & release egg	P&RL	14	350
To egg carton	TE	17	367

CLOCK OR METER READING: 0, 20, 40, 60, 80, 100, 120, 140, 160, 180, 200, 220, 240, 260, 280, 300, 320, 340, 360

Right Hand

Accrued Time	Time	Sym.	Right Hand Description
17	17	TE	To egg carton
40	23	G&PP	Grasp & pre-position egg
56	16	TL	To egg tray
71	15	P&RL	Position & release egg
82	11	TE	To egg carton
132	50	G&PP	Grasp & pre-position egg
151	19	TL	To egg tray
161	10	P&RL	Position & release egg
178	17	TE	To egg carton
189	11	G&PP	Grasp & pre-position egg
210	21	TL	To egg tray
219	9	P&RL	Position & release egg
231	12	TE	To egg carton
252	21	G&PP	Grasp & pre-position egg
266	14	TL	To egg tray
281	15	P&RL	Position & release egg
295	14	TE	To egg carton
317	22	G&PP	Grasp & pre-position egg
336	19	TL	To egg tray
350	14	P&RL	Position & release egg
361	11	TE	To egg carton

Left hand	Symbol	Time	Cumulative	Scale	Cumulative	Time	Symbol	Right hand
Grasp & pre-position egg	G&PP	23		380		29	G&PP	Grasp & pre-position egg
			390		390			
To egg tray	TL	17		400		17	TL	To egg tray
			407		407			
Position & release egg	P&RL	18		420		18	P&RL	Position & release egg
			425		425			
To starting position	TE	20		440		20	TE	To starting position
			445		445			
				460				

Left Hand Summary

%	Symbol	Time
27%	TE	118
16%	G	71.5
16%	PP	71.5
23%	TL	102
9%	P	41
9%	RL	41

Right Hand Summary

Time	Symbol	%
102	TE	23.0%
78	G	17.5%
78	PP	17.5%
106	TL	24.0%
40.5	P	9.0%
40.5	RL	9.0%

2. Ask yourself again, *Am I the right person to do this job?* Do I have a natural aptitude for it, mental, physical and emotional? What amount of knowledge does the job require, how much dexterity and strength? What mental blocks do I have which can be removed?

If the answer is yes—that is, if you are the person to do the job, ask yourself, Do I get the results I want? Is the job satisfying? Is my pace right? Do I get overtired? Can I rest in some way during the job?

3. If the answer is no, and you feel you are not cast for this role, what can you do about it? Can you do some other work and send out some of the housework, or hire help? Can you lay plans for doing this in the future, if not now? If you have help, do you know how to direct the helper? Learn to give instructions. Your process chart will aid you in this. By listing all the steps in the process, you will learn to describe a job in writing so that another person can do it. Unclear directions can result in all kinds of inefficiency, from mere annoyance to real accidents. Just take a look at the directions on a package of prepared pudding and remember that these directions have to be written so that people of every level of intelligence can follow them, and you will get an idea of the importance of clear, simple job descriptions.

Housework offers so much variety that it is possible to be quite flexible. If there are parts of it you don't like, you can give them to someone else, or you can improve your attitude toward them by changing the time, place or method of doing them.

Some people like to work in the morning. They want to get up early and get everything done fast. Others do best at night. If they are forced to change their hours, fatigue, anger, poor quality and quantity, even accidents may result.

People differ very much in their approach to work. Some plunge into activity, others enjoy the spectator's role or that of the sidewalk superintendent. Some prefer to stand at work, and may walk and even run at jobs. Others prefer to sit, and are good subjects to teach to work sitting.

Some people are so fond of activity that they enjoy it even if it accomplishes nothing of tangible value. They must always be doing something. They will knit or crochet things no one wants, or put fancy icings on cakes for no good reason. Others resent jobs which they consider don't get them anywhere. They hate dusting only to see a new film of dust appear. They hate cooking and washing dishes because it just has to be done all over again.

One woman will feel that in cooking a dinner she is really achieving a result, or that in knitting a sweater she is making something tangible. Another will argue that for a few dollars she can buy a prepared meal or a ready-made sweater. She may consider that mass production is more efficient, and that she had better save her physical energy for teaching school or writing a book.

If the job doesn't seem worth while to you, find out what other work seems better. But if it is merely a matter of saving energy and preventing fatigue, don't give it up but find out what kind of relaxation it allows, and what kind you require. Some people are rested by a change of posture, doing part of a job standing and part sitting. Others are helped by putting their feet up, still others by lying flat for a few minutes.

To eliminate all possible activity, remember: never run when you can walk, never walk when you can stand, never stand when you can sit, never sit when you can lie down.

Try to remove causes of pressure or tension. Some people think they like pressure. They say, "I have to have a deadline to work against." They let the work pile up, get at a job as late as possible, like to do it at top speed. Is this good? Well, if it disturbs no one else and doesn't seem to harm the worker, it may be all right. But then that person must be depended on to get the job done since other people usually can't fit into his schedule.

Sometimes a treat ahead may galvanize every member of a family to work as a team at top speed. For example, the family may decide on the spur of the moment to go on a camping trip.

Food has to be prepared, equipment taken out, the car made ready, the children have to get their homework done. This is fun once in a while. But usually tension is not a good taskmaster.

The process chart is a good instrument for cutting out tension because it shows so clearly where you are wasting time and motion. If you feel that it is too complicated for your purposes, of course you can make it as simple as you choose. Remember that it is only a record, showing what has been done and what changes have been made, and a record can be anything. It can be a drawing or a written description, a chart or a combination of charts. It can even be a moving picture.

A great deal of use is being made of films nowadays. A camera records every motion—many that the eye would miss entirely. It is useful because it can be run as often as you like. An engineer could not get a worker to stand at a bench and saw a piece of wood twenty times. But he can take a film of the job and then run it twenty or a hundred times, backward or forward, slowly or quickly. He can stop it at any point and then run any part of it again.

Then he can analyze the job, break it down into operations, delays, storages, and so on. He can make a process chart from the film.

Moving pictures are a great help if you want to observe a job being done by several people at once, and they are fine for showing workers what they themselves have been doing. People who don't visualize well, or who can't take verbal or written instructions and translate them into actions, will know what is meant when they see the thing done.

In industry, films are used to get a detailed breakdown of the very smallest finger movements. This is called *micromotion study*, and it is being used more and more by home economists to find better ways of doing routine jobs.

Just as a job as a whole is broken down into five main divisions, so cycles of hand and body movements have been broken down into seventeen separate subdivisions called *therbligs* (a coined word made by spelling backward the name of the engineer who first identified them). A special word is used to describe each motion, and each word has its own symbol. Thus, to describe the motion that the hand makes in taking hold of something, the word "grasp" is used, with the symbol "G." The motion of the empty hand in reaching for an object is called "Transport empty," with the symbol "TE." The motion of the hand carrying something is called "Transport loaded–TL."

Below you will see a complete list of the therbligs.

THERBLIG SYMBOLS AND DEFINITIONS *

1. *Search* (*Sh*).

Search refers to that part of the cycle during which the eyes or the hands are hunting or groping for the object. Search begins when the eyes or hands begin to hunt for the object and ends when the object has been found.

2. *Select* (*St*).

Select refers to the choice of one object from among several. In many cases it is difficult if not impossible to determine where the boundaries lie between search and select. For this reason it is often the practice to combine them, referring to both as the one therblig *select*.

Using this broader definition, *select* then refers to the hunting and locating of one object from among several. Select therefore begins when the eyes or hands begin to hunt for the object and ends when the desired object has been located.

Example: Locating a particular pencil in a box containing pencils, pens and miscellaneous articles.

* Reprinted with permission from Ralph M. Barnes, *Motion and Time Study*, John Wiley & Sons, Inc., New York, 1949, pp. 95 ff.

3. *Grasp* (*G*).

Grasp refers to taking hold of an object, closing the fingers around it preparatory to picking it up, holding it or manipulating it. Grasp begins when the hand or fingers first make contact with the object and ends when the hand has obtained control of it.

Example: Closing the fingers around the pen on the desk.

4. *Transport Empty* (*TE*).

Transport Empty refers to moving the empty hand in reaching for an object. It is assumed that the hand moves without resistance toward or away from the object. Transport empty begins when the hand begins to move without load or resistance and ends when the hand stops moving.

Example: Moving the empty hand to grasp a pen on the desk.

5. *Transport Loaded* (*TL*).

Transport Loaded refers to moving an object from one place to another. The object may be carried in the hands or fingers or it may be moved from one place to another by sliding, dragging, or pushing it along. Transport loaded also refers to moving the empty hand against resistance. Transport loaded begins when the hand begins to move an object or encounter resistance and ends when the hand stops moving.

Example: Carrying the pen from the desk set to the letter to be signed.

6. *Hold* (*H*).

Hold refers to the retention of an object after it has been grasped, no movement of the object taking place. Hold begins when the movement of the object stops and ends with the start of the next therblig.

Example: Holding bolt in one hand while assembling a washer on to it with the other.

7. *Release Load* (*RL*).

Release Load refers to letting go of the object. Release load begins when the object starts to leave the hand and ends when the object has been completely separated from the hand or fingers.

Example: Letting go of the pen after it has been placed on the desk.

8. *Position* (*P*).

Position consists of turning or locating an object in such a way that it will be properly oriented to fit into the location for which it is intended. It is possible to position an object during the motion *transport loaded.* The carpenter, for example, may turn the nail into position for using while he is carrying it to the board into which it will be driven. Position begins when the hand begins to turn or locate the object and ends when the object has been placed in the desired position or location.

Example: Lining up a door key preparatory to inserting it in the keyhole.

9. *Pre-position* (*PP*).

Pre-position refers to locating an object in a predetermined place or locating it in the correct position for some subsequent motion. Pre-position is the same as position except that the object is located in the approximate position in which it will be needed later. Usually a holder, bracket or special container of some kind is used for holding the object in a way that permits it to be grasped easily in the position in which it will be used. *Pre-position* is the abbreviated term used for *pre-position for the next operation.*

Example: Locating or lining up the pen above the desk set

holder prior to releasing it. (The pen may then be grasped in approximately the correct position for writing. This eliminates the therblig *position* that would be required to turn the pen to the correct writing position if it were resting flat on the desk when grasped.)

10. Inspect (I).

Inspect consists of examining an object to determine whether or not it complies with standard size, shape, color, or other qualities previously determined. The inspection may employ sight, hearing, touch, odor or taste. Inspect is predominantly a mental reaction and may occur simultaneously with other therbligs. Inspect begins when the eyes or other parts of the body begin to examine the object and ends when the examination has been completed.

Example: Visual examination of pearl buttons in the final sorting operation.

11. Assemble (A).

Assemble consists of placing one object into or on another object with which it becomes an integral part. Assemble begins as the hand starts to move the part into its place in the assembly and ends when the hand has completed the assembly.

Example: Placing cap on mechanical pencil.

12. Disassemble (DA).

Disassemble consists of separating one object from another object of which it is an integral part. Disassemble begins when the hand starts to remove one part from the assembly and ends when the hand has separated the part completely from the remainder of the assembly.

Example: Removing the cap from mechanical pencil.

13. Use (U).

Use consists of manipulating a tool, device, or piece of apparatus for the purpose for which it was intended. Use may refer to an almost infinite number of particular cases. It represents the motion for which the preceding motions have been more or less preparatory and for which the ones that follow are supplementary. Use begins when the hand starts to manipulate the tool or device and ends when the hand ceases the application.

Example: Writing one's signature in signing a letter (use pen) or painting an object with spray gun (use spray gun).

14. Unavoidable Delay (UD).

Unavoidable Delay refers to a delay beyond the control of the operator. Unavoidable delay may result from either of the following causes:

A. A failure or interruption in the process.

B. A delay caused by an arrangement of the operation which prevents one part of the body from working while other body members are busy.

Unavoidable delay begins when the hand stops its activity and ends when activity is resumed.

Example: If the left hand made a long transport motion to the left and the right hand simultaneously made a very short transport motion to the right, an unavoidable delay would occur at the end of the right-hand transport in order to bring the two hands into balance.

15. Avoidable Delay (AD).

Avoidable Delay begins when the prescribed sequence of motions is interrupted and ends when the standard work method is resumed.

Example: The operator stops all hand motions.

16. Plan (Pn).

Plan refers to a mental reaction which precedes the physical movement, that is, deciding how to proceed with the job. Plan begins at the point where the operator begins to work out the next step of the operation and ends when the procedure to be followed has been determined.

Example: An operator assembling a complex mechanism, deciding which part should be assembled next.

17. Rest for overcoming fatigue (R).

Rest for overcoming fatigue is a fatigue or delay factor or allowance provided to permit the worker to recover from the fatigue incurred by his work. Rest begins when the operator stops working and ends when work is resumed.

When the engineer wants to make a micromotion study he has the worker placed as he would normally be for the job, with a clock or chronometer and his materials and tools in front of him. Then the film is taken of the worker doing the job. It is usually a repetitive job which can be divided into cycles. In a factory, it might be putting together some small article like a nut and bolt assembly. In a home, or a home economics laboratory, it might be making salads.

The engineer watches the film being run through once for the left hand, then again for the right hand, making a record all the time of what each hand is doing, in terms of therbligs, and giving the clock reading to show how long each therblig took in seconds, fractions of a second, or frames of the motion picture, which are approximately 1/1000 of a minute each for a movie camera that makes 16 pictures per second. If the chronometer is set to go round twenty times a minute, each division on its face will amount to 1/2000 of a minute (since there are 100 divisions). This is known as a wink.

From the film he makes a list of the successive movements for each hand. This is called a micromotion transfer sheet.

Thus if a worker is making salads, having two trays and a pan of vegetables in front of her and a pile of plates at one side, the micromotion transfer sheet might read like this:

LEFT HAND			RIGHT HAND		
TL	Finished salad to tray	8 winks	TE	To table	
RL	Release plate	2 "	UD	Waiting	20 winks
TE	Pan of lettuce	16 "	G	Plate	10 "
G	Leaf of lettuce	8 "	TL	To tray	10 "
TL	Next plate	4 "			
RL	Release leaf	2 "			

In order to show the time required for each movement and what the two hands are doing at all times, a *simultaneous motion* or *simo chart* is constructed.

A study of the chart will show the engineer where time is wasted in *avoidable delay*, when one hand is idle while the other works; where *transport empty* could be cut down; where *search* and *select* could be speeded up by a better arrangement of the work place; where *grasp* could be made easier by having the parts in better containers; where *release load* can be cut out by having a tool pre-positioned; where *inspect* can be improved by better light.

Though each therblig lasts for only a few thousandths of a minute, the result of the whole study may be a saving of 400 winks for each assembly, whether it be a salad or nuts and bolts, and when you consider that this means the worker can make 20% more salads, you will see that the study is worth while where there is any large-scale activity.

In the section entitled "Charts" following page 86 you will see the micromotion transfer sheets and simo charts for the original and improved methods of transferring eggs from a carton to a refrigerator tray.* In the original method, the left hand was used only for holding while the right hand did the work. In the improved method, both hands worked. There was a saving of 44%.

Whether this sort of thing is worth while to you in your home or not is for you to decide. At the very least, it can't help increasing your respect for the value of time. But more than that, you may find it a rewarding piece of research. There is a vast field waiting to be studied, and you may become so enthusiastic that you will go ahead and make it your life work.

But even if you don't, there is still a lot that can be done with your home movie camera and projector. First of all, this will be a family project. How could the family fail to be interested in setting the stage for a film study of dishwashing, or the morning rush for the bathroom, or washing the car, or baking a cake. Let the children take the pictures. Get a film of each member of the family doing the job and see what one does that can be copied, and what another does that should be avoided. This is a good way for people to teach each other. It is a fine way to illustrate traffic problems. Now you can see why they bump into each other—that table is in the wrong place and too many people are trying to do the same thing at the same time.

You can examine your pace. It is fun to run the film at double its normal speed to show how silly it looks for everybody to be galloping hither and yon, and you can slow it down to show how snails walk when they're doing a job they don't like.

Johnny will find that movies show what's wrong with his batting and pitching. Mary can see her progress in ballet, and Father can study his golf stroke, and then they can all pitch in and tell Mother how to do her dusting or canning.

In addition to showing your own films, you can buy or rent

* Courtesy of Handicapped Housewife's Workshop, University of Connecticut.

films about all sorts of subjects from sports to baby-tending.

The Department of Extension Teaching and Information at the New York State College of Agriculture at Ithaca, New York, rents or lends films to schools, Granges, service clubs and farm and home organizations. Find out from your state college what films they have and how you can get them.

The United States Department of Agriculture has placed films in co-operating film libraries in all states. You can write to the Office of Information of the Department in Washington, D.C., to find out what films are available in your state and where the state film library is.

There are films on farming, industry, conservation, family life, clothing, homemaking, food, entertainment, and many other subjects. Many of them are loaned free. For others there is a small charge.

The Communication Materials Center at Columbia University, 413 West 117 Street, New York, N.Y., has a large library of films which can be rented and sent by mail.

You can invite the neighbors in, form a group of movie fans, and make it a community project as well as a family one.

Even if you don't make your own simo charts, you may find the therbligs useful in writing job directions, and the standing order will look very professional if you use words like grasp, position, assemble, select.

If you have no movie camera, there are still things you can do. You can take pictures with an ordinary box camera, which will show a great deal that you don't see with the naked eye. A picture will illustrate the stoop in your back from a too low work table or the expression of strain on your face from inadequate light. It will show books, mending, groceries, papers piled up because there is no proper work center.

Be sure to write all the necessary information on the back of the photograph or on a label underneath—date, place, explanation and statement of what is needed. After the improvements have been made take another picture, with a legend giving costs, measurements, and the names of those who worked on the project.

Mount these exhibits on the wall alongside your string and process charts. But don't ever think of them as the last word. Regard them rather as an interim report, and keep looking for the One Best Way.

Chapter 5

Making Changes—Work Methods and Your Work Place

In the course of the previous chapter you saw how certain very simple changes in storage and sequence of jobs helped you to save time and energy.

This is only the beginning. The engineer's time and motion study may lead him from a few shifts in the order of jobs to a drastic revamping of the whole plant. Similarly the motion study you make in your own kitchen may open the way to more changes than you ever dreamed of.

Many people think of changes in terms of buying. Look at the magazine articles on kitchen efficiency. Frequently you'll see a "before" picture of a drab, out-dated kitchen, followed by an "after" shot of a gorgeous, streamlined room full of brand new equipment.

Ask your neighbor, "How do you think your work could be made easier?" Nine times out of ten she'll say, "Well, if I could get some new furniture, or if we could remodel the house—but of course we can't afford it."

And there she sticks. Nine out of ten of us *can't* afford to buy new equipment or appliances or have the house remodeled, even though it would be nice to do. But there is a great deal we *can* do and *should* do without spending a penny. Indeed the first and most important changes in our ways of working cost nothing; yet they are basic, and even if we *are* planning to refurnish and redecorate, we shouldn't do it without considering these simple and vital principles.

They are called the *Principles of Motion Economy*.

You saw in the chapter on process charts that there are four chief means of improving jobs:

a. By eliminating all unnecessary work.
b. By combining operations or elements.
c. By changing the sequence of operations.
d. By simplifying the necessary operations.

These things can be done in various ways:

a. By developing better work methods.
b. By improving your work place.
c. By using better tools and supplies.
d. By changing the places where you keep your tools and supplies —better storage.
e. By changing the whole layout, including working conditions.
f. By improving maintenance.

You may want to do all these things at once and not know where to start. This is natural because they are all interrelated. As you look around at your home with a view to making some changes, your eye may light on a sink that is too low, on a paring knife that is never sharp enough, on a drawer that sticks, on a shelf that you can't reach. You may be loath to bake a cake because it means getting out so many utensils and putting them all back. You may put off mending because it strains your eyes. What is the least common denominator of all these things?

Each one involves a faulty *work method.* They may involve faulty tools and arrangements too, but first and foremost comes the work method. And the first and most important work method is the proper use of your body.

Consider your muscles as tools and use the right ones for the job you are doing.

If you are painting, for instance, you don't, in order to get extra good results, use three brushes at once and bear down on them as though they were scrubbing brushes. You use only the

brush that fits the job and you use it only as hard as necessary.

It is the same with your body. The reason why it is bad to wash dishes at a low sink is that in addition to the muscles needed to do the actual work of washing dishes, you are making other muscles work unnecessarily to hold your body in a strained position.

When you reach too far forward across a table to cut a dress, or when you bend over from the hips to pick up the baby instead of bending your knees, you put extra strain on your muscles and make them do things they shouldn't have to do. In this way you get needlessly fatigued.

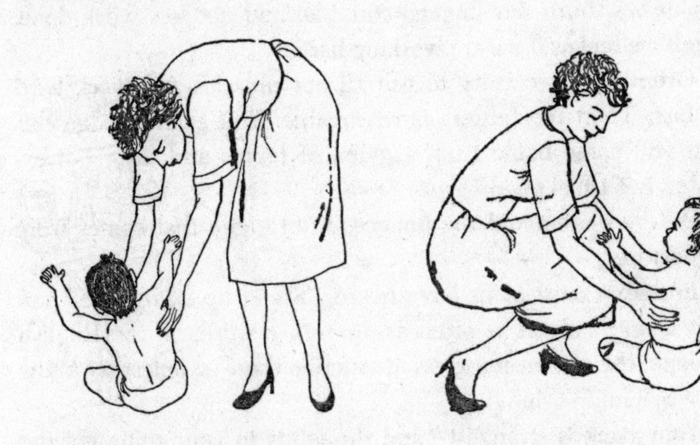

What is fatigue?

Like any machine, the body needs energy in order to work. This is supplied by the sugars which are brought to the different muscles by the blood stream. Along with the sugars, the blood stream also brings oxygen, and the sugars are oxidized (burned up as fuel), giving off energy and waste products, just the way a steam engine gives off energy and waste products.

In the case of the engine, the waste products are smoke and ashes. In the case of the body, the waste products are carbon dioxide and lactic acid. The carbon dioxide is taken away by the blood stream and breathed out by the lungs. But the lactic acid stays in the muscles until some more oxygen comes along and converts it back into sugar.

If the body is working at a moderate pace, and in a well-ventilated place so that there is plenty of oxygen, the amount of lactic acid is kept down and the muscles can go on working with little fatigue. But if we go full steam ahead, or if all the muscles are working at once, the fatigue products accumulate and we feel tired. When this happens the nerves that control the muscles are the first things to be affected. They just can't stand too many fatigue products. That's why, when we get tired, we make mistakes, drop dishes, burn our fingers, stumble, and get less work done, though we feel as if we are working harder.

Often it is necessary to use all our muscles and work hard and fast. Then the fatigue is reasonable. You acknowledge this when you come home from a game of tennis and say, "I'm exhausted but I feel good."

But you can avoid the unnecessary fatigue that comes from bad posture.

Probably most of us have heard, "Stand up straight! Sit up! Don't slump!" about as often as any other words in the English language. It is the most useless instruction there is, unless we know *why* we shouldn't slump.

Your back is strongest (and the joints in your spine get the most protection) when it is straight. If you walk with your chin sticking out in front and your hips sticking out behind, or your head and shoulders sagging forward, your body will be out of balance and there will be great strain on the small muscles and ligaments. So, when you stand, keep your head up, your chin in, your chest up, your abdomen in, and your hips well under you.

When you sit, don't slump or sag sideways. Sit well back in your chair (never slouch with the small of your back perched on the front edge of the chair), and keep your body straight from hips to neck. Lean forward from the hips, not the shoulders or waist.

Your large leg muscles are very strong—the strongest in your body. So when you walk, swing your legs from the hip, not the knee. Point your toes straight ahead.

Never climb stairs by dragging yourself up with your knees bent and your body leaning forward. Stair climbing takes 1336% more energy than lying still. You don't want to increase it by doing it wrong. Keep your body erect and give the job of weightlifting to the strong leg muscles.

You should lift with your legs too. Bend your knees, get your body under the load and then straighten your legs to lift.

If you have to push a chest of drawers or shove a sticking door, brace your feet, push against the floor and use your big muscles plus your whole body weight. When you pull, brace your feet, bend your knees and let your body weight do the work.

Good health is a very important requirement for good work habits. If you are constantly fatigued, you should have a check-up before you go any farther. But if your health turns out to be fine, perhaps a little motion study is all you need.

Engineers have found in factories that properly spaced *rest periods* increase the amount of work done in a day. When the engineer makes a graph of a worker's output, he finds that it starts at a low point in the morning, and then rises. This indicates a warming up period. About the middle of the morning it reaches its high point and stays level for a while. Then it starts to go down. This means the worker is getting tired. If he has a rest just at the point where the curve starts to descend, he will work better afterward.

So learn to rest. Find out when your peak of fatigue comes. In one experiment, about a hundred housewives were questioned about this. The greatest number said they felt most tired at about two in the afternoon, and again at about seven in the evening. If you agree, then these would be good times for a rest. After lunch, and again after dinner, lie down and stretch your arms over your head. Stretch your whole body, and then relax completely. This need not be for a long time. Only ten minutes of it will do you a lot of good.

Of course if you are doing sedentary work, like sewing or writing, perhaps a rest would consist of changing to another type of activity—going out for a short walk or working in the garden, or even sweeping the floor.

Watch your *pace*. Fatigue products have a chance to be removed when you are not working too fast. If you go at a moderate, steady pace you can keep going much longer than if you rush about.

Remember that the proper pace isn't always the same. It's slower when the heat and the humidity are high. In the tropics, nobody thinks of dashing from one job to another as we do in the cooler climates. Life in the city is always more hectic than in the

country. Try not to let yourself get swept away in the current. You can use your time economically and still not have to run for the bus or the train. Remind yourself that another one is bound to come along. If you are always having to dash for trains or rush for appointments, it may mean your schedule needs reorganization.

Rhythm is related to pace. Rhythm means regular repetition of motions. If you can get an easy natural rhythm into jobs that consist of a lot of similar motions, you will save energy and get the work done with less strain.

To help you get rhythm into your work, try to use smooth, continuous, free-sweeping movements rather than sharp, straight ones. It takes less energy to move your arm around in a circle, if you are dusting, or in a smooth curved pattern, if you are ironing, than to move it at random in choppy zigzag lines, because in the

latter you use extra muscles to stop the arm at the end of the movement and pull it back to its starting point, whereas in a circular movement you use the same set of muscles and don't have to overcome the momentum of the arm.

Momentum is something that can be used to hinder or help you. If you are using a tool, you can make the weight of the tool do part of the work and relieve your muscles. The weight of an iron, for instance, can do the work for you if you merely guide it back and forth. If the iron is too light, you must use your arm muscles to press down on the cloth.

If you are folding sheets and laying them in a pile, you will get less fatigued if you lightly drop or toss them, thus letting the weight of the sheets help in the job, than if you carefully lay each one down, making your muscles overcome the momentum of the sheets.

Try to use both hands for a job whenever possible, and balance the movements of your hands by using motions that are equal and opposite in direction. You know that in swimming, the breast stroke is the easiest to do because the arms are making equal and opposite motions.

Just try an exercise like this: pound on the table with one hand and at the same time move the other hand back and forth sideways. Or pat your head with one hand and rub your tummy in a circular motion with the other. Quite difficult!

Apply the principle of using both hands in opposite directions to kneading dough, washing clothes, dusting, scrubbing; use two dusting mitts and even two scrubbing brushes. It may take a while to get your left hand trained, but it's a habit worth forming.

Use other parts of the body besides hands and arms whenever possible. Move a chair or a stool with your foot. Open or close a door with a gentle push of your foot or knee.

The eyes are in use most of the time. Eye motions are among the most fatiguing of all, since they are so completely automatic that we don't notice them. Rest your eyes occasionally. Notice whether the muscles around them are tense. Sometimes your forehead and eyelids are quite tight and you don't realize it. Close your eyes and take a few deep breaths, or lie down for five minutes with a wet washcloth across your closed eyelids.

Try to avoid situations where you have to look quickly back and forth a great many times. If you prop your cookbook up in front of you, for instance, rather than at one side, you can simply raise your eyes in order to consult it.

From learning how to use the muscles, we learn how to arrange our environment so as to save work for the muscles.

This may read rather strangely to you. We are so accustomed to being told to exercise so as to have movie-star figures, that the idea of using as little energy as possible may sound most peculiar. These suggestions are not meant to turn you into a mollusk. They were worked out for normal people, with the usual amount of energy. Their purpose is to conserve that energy so as to increase output, or to enable you to do more things.

As we said before, there are many people who enjoy vigorous activity. There are others who need exercise for reducing or to train certain muscles, or as physiotherapy, to restore weakened muscles to health. These people can make good use of strenuous work like sweeping, dusting, scrubbing or washing clothes.

At the other end of the scale there are people who can do much less than the normal person. Some have limited energy at all times—old people, or those with heart trouble or tuberculosis. Some have limited energy at certain specific times, during pregnancy or after an illness. And others are handicapped in one way or another and need special devices such as wheel chairs, crutches, ambulance cots or walkers to help them get about. Studies have been made to show what the handicapped woman can do to help herself and keep her home running smoothly. Some of them show the most amazing ingenuity.

One woman who was confined to a wheel chair and bed did the cooking, set and cleared the table, ironed and sewed for her family. Another woman had a leg injury which made walking and standing difficult. Nevertheless she managed to do all her housework, including laundry and cleaning. All this was accomplished by careful planning of equipment, schedules and layout, and by simplified work methods.*

The Institute of Physical Medicine and Rehabilitation in New York has done a great deal of work to help disabled homemakers.

The New York Heart Association has set up a model kitchen to show how all the principles of work simplification and human engineering that we have been discussing can be used to help the woman who *must* take it easy to stay on the job.

When a woman *can't* climb stairs or reach or lift or carry, it's obvious that we have to use our best ideas to help her. But even if you're in perfect health and strong as a horse, such ideas can help you too.

You must classify yourself as to how much you can do, and adapt your surroundings, equipment, tools and methods to meet your own needs.

Think about the amount of use you demand from different parts of your body. Work requires action. Your eyes are in use most of your waking hours. Your hands and arms are in use much of the time; your shoulders, trunk and legs, proportionately less. The larger the motion, and the more weight involved, the greater the fatigue. This does not contradict the principle that you should use large muscles to do heavy work. It means that you shouldn't use large muscles where small ones will do.

Here is how engineers classify motions, according to the

* Julia S. Judson, *Home Management Aids for Women with Physical Difficulties*, unpublished thesis, Ohio State University, 1949, pp. 68 ff.

amount of time and effort required and the amount of fatigue caused:

1. Finger motions only
2. Motions involving fingers and wrist
3. Motions involving fingers, wrist and forearm
4. Motions involving fingers, wrist, forearm and upper arm
5. Motions involving fingers, wrist, forearm, upper arm, shoulder and possibly the entire body

When you think about this list, you will see why your tools and materials should be as close as possible to the place where they will be used, and why we use labor-saving devices. These are work methods which are extensions of the use of the body, just as a stirring spoon is an extension of your hand.

When an engineer designs a tool to save labor, he tries to make one that takes the lowest classification of motions. Thus, an electric mixer on which you just press a button with your finger uses fewer muscles than an egg-beater which is worked by your hand and forearm. The beater, however, is an improvement over your grandmother's method of whipping eggs with a fork on a platter, which used the whole arm, and a lot more time.

The long-handled dust pan and brush can be worked with the arms alone. The short-handled ones require that you bend over, using back and leg muscles as well.

The same thing applies to ovens and refrigerators. The old-fashioned kind that stood well up on legs was really kinder to your back than many of the modern streamlined ones that sit down near the floor so that you practically have to get on your knees to look inside.

A tool that can be used with a light touch is more efficient than one that requires pressure. For peeling vegetables, the two-edged oscillating parer is more useful than a regular knife. A sharp knife is better than a dull one. A smoothly oiled wheel is better than a rusty one. Drawers and doors that glide open easily are better for your muscles than those that have to be yanked and kicked.

Sliding shelves and revolving shelves that bring their contents to you require less muscle use than stationary ones on which you have to reach for things.

We store our tools and supplies in *definite and fixed places.* This means we don't need to exert extra effort to hunt around for the spoon or the salt-shaker, or run all over the kitchen wondering

where we laid it down. We can simply form the habit of reaching out for the tool, and if we have already formed the habit of putting it back where it belongs, the reaching hand will find it. This eliminates a lot of fatigue.

We store things *at the point of first use* and we use *one-motion storage* as much as possible, thus eliminating the many extra motions of going to get something, reaching for something, moving something out of the way.

We design our work places as *work centers.* This means that all the tools and supplies we need for a particular job are kept at the place where that job is done. Thus in the kitchen you will have a sink center where you wash dishes, prepare vegetables, get water for cooking, drain foods, and do some laundry. You will have a range center where the cooking is done, and a mix center, where

you prepare food for cooking, mix cakes, fix salads. At each place you store the pots and pans, the supplies and tools you use there. Proper storage is an important work method which will be discussed more fully in the next chapter.

The counter at which you work should be of a comfortable height. In case you don't realize how important this is, try sitting in a low chair and beating some batter in a bowl with a long-handled spoon on the table in front of you. Your arms will ache from working on a surface that is too high. Then try washing dishes in a sink that's too low. (If you are lucky enough to have a sink just the right height, stand on a telephone book for the experiment.) See if you don't get a pain in the neck. This is what many women stand for without even realizing it.

An experiment was made to see how much energy it took to wash dishes at tables of different heights. This is the way it worked out: when the table was 25.6 inches from the floor, it took 30 calories per hour. When the table was 39.4 inches from the floor, it took 24.4 calories per hour. When the table was 33 inches from the floor, it took 20.3 calories.

The too low table took the most energy, the too high one somewhat less, and the 33-inch table, which is about the right sink height for the average woman, took the least.

Women were asked to work at ironing boards of different heights for 3-hour periods for several days. Those who complained of backache when using the 31-inch board felt a lot better with a 34- or 35-inch board.*

How can you find out what is correct work-table height? There are several ways.

Take a chopping board and a knife and a head of cabbage. Stand at your counter or table and make cole slaw. Or do some other job that requires a short-handled tool. You should be able to stand with your arms comfortably relaxed from the shoulders, without stooping, and you should not have to raise your hands above the level of your elbows. If you can work in this position the counter height is correct for you.

If you are about 5 feet 4 inches tall, a counter height of 36 inches is just about right for vegetable preparation, and for range

* Elaine E. Knowles, *Some Effects of the Height of Ironing Surface on the Worker*, Cornell University Agricultural Experiment Station, Bulletin 833, 1946.

and drainboards.

Now take an egg-beater and a bowl and pretend to make scrambled eggs. Or use some other long-handled tool, like a stirring spoon, and beat up a make-believe cake. You will probably find that a work surface 32 inches high is the most comfortable for your mix center and sink base.

If you sit in an ordinary chair while working, you would probably prefer a table only 25 inches high, the height of a typewriter table, for your mixing.

The measurements given above are for a woman of "average" height—5 feet 4. But maybe you don't happen to be 5 feet 4. If you are 5 feet 2, or 5 feet 6, or 5 feet 8, these measurements, of course, won't suit you.

An accurate way to find your proper work height is this: stand erect, and have somebody measure the distance from your elbow to the floor. Your work counter should be 2 or 3 inches lower than this, so that you will be able to work without raising your hand above elbow level. If you are 5 feet 6, for instance, your elbow level may be 41 inches above the floor. Then your drainboards, counter and range should be 38 inches high, and your mix center and sink well should be 34 inches high.*

Obviously you can't always remake your kitchen. There are some things you can do, though. If your work counter is too low, raise its height by building a row of shallow drawers on top of it. If your counters and tables are too high for long-handled tools, try beating things in the sink well, or rig up a pull-out lap board, and work sitting. Or use a portable table that is lower than your regular table. Or stand on a rack to raise yourself high enough for the table. Or sit on a stool or chair which brings you to the right height.

The sink is frequently too low, less often too high. It is

* Figures are adapted from Cornell Extension Bulletin 703, Mary Koll Heiner and Helen E. McCullough, *Kitchen Cupboards that Simplify Storage*, July, 1951. Also *Heart of the Home*, Pictorial Supplement, American Heart Association, New York, N.Y.

seldom just what you want, and it is the hardest thing in the kitchen to adjust. If your counters are 36 inches high, your sink drainboards are usually placed to match, and this means that if your sink is 6 inches deep, its bottom surface is too low for comfort. Build a wooden rack to set in the sink, and place your dishpan or mixing bowl on it. This will serve the double purpose of adjusting height and saving your sink from scratches. If you plan to wash dishes directly in the sink well, it might pay you to have the sink itself raised. Just think of those 135,000 dishes you have to wash in five years!

If your sink is too high, stand on a rack, if you can be sure you won't stumble in stepping on or off. You'll have the trouble of getting up and down, but it will save backaches.

A stove can be raised on wooden blocks, but can't be lowered. So if the stove is too high, you may have to put up with it.

Your work chair should be of such a height as to let you sit as you stand, with your arms and shoulders relaxed, and without raising the hands above the level of the elbows. There should be a foot rest so that your feet don't dangle, and there should be a back rest that supports you right in the middle of the back, not at the shoulders. Try to get an adjustable chair that you can raise or lower to suit yourself. If this is impossible, put a firm cushion on the seat, or cut off the legs to make the chair seat the right height.

Researchers have found that the ideal chair has a seat that is wide enough (16 or 17 inches) but not too deep (not more than 13 or 14 inches from back to front).* This is for the average worker. If you vary much in height or weight you will have to experiment until you find one that suits you. Too deep a seat will tend to stop circulation of the blood by pressing under the thighs just behind the knees. The seat should slope slightly backward, so you don't slide forward. You can improvise by making a pad

* Ralph M. Barnes, *Motion and Time Study,* John Wiley & Sons, Inc., New York, 1949, p. 278.

for the seat, thicker at the front and thinner in back, and you can pad the back rest so that it supports your spine without making you lean forward too far.

Your chair and counter should be of such a height that you can sit or stand as you choose, and still work without stooping or raising the hand above the level of the elbow. It is very restful to be able to get up or sit down in this way, especially if you are doing a long job.

Ideally you should be able to sit with your knees under the table, and there should be plenty of leg room. There ought to be from six to ten inches of space between the chair seat and the under side of the table. This isn't always possible in kitchens, where the space under counters is generally used for storage. This makes you sit sidewise. It is possible to get a very good crick in the back or neck this way. Try to have at least one working counter or table or shelf where you can sit with your knees under the surface.

To find how high your work chair should be, have someone measure you from elbow to floor while you are standing. Then sit down and measure again from elbow to floor. The distance should be the same whether you are sitting or standing. If you measure 41 inches standing and 35 inches sitting, your chair is too low. It ought to be 6 inches higher.

The depth of your work counter is important too. If it is too deep you will find that you don't use the entire surface to work on, but most likely keep on it a lot of miscellaneous stuff which doesn't belong there, collects dust, and gradually works its way forward and takes over the surface you do want to use. It is much better to store nothing on your working surface, and to have a shelf for supplies on the wall behind it, with small tools hung on hooks on the wall itself. If your counter is too deep, build a little step at the back. This will make the counter narrower and provide a platform for storage so that the counter itself is kept clear.

You know how cluttered grocery store counters get. The storekeeper piles up a variety of cookies, candies, jars of jam, and other special offers right where you stand while he totals up your purchases. As you wait, you see these things and add one or two to your list. Or your little boy or girl starts to beg, "Mama, buy me this!" And often you do. This may be good business but gradually the counter becomes so stacked with merchandise that the grocer has no room to work. You get a real feeling of relief when you go into a store that looks uncluttered.

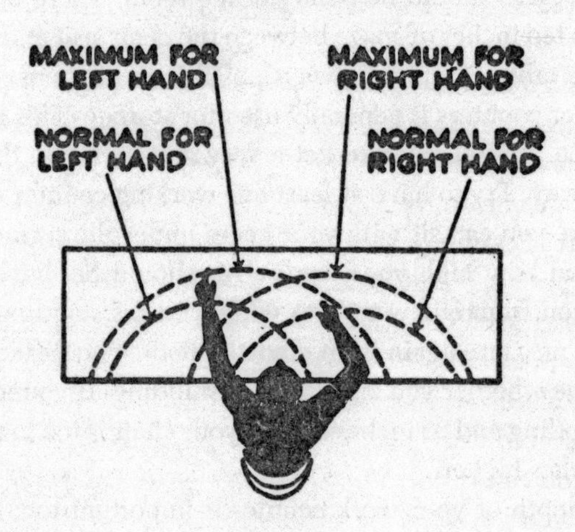

It's the same in your kitchen. Keep your work surface free for work and don't use it for storage.

To see how deep your work counter should be, sit down at a table of comfortable height which is covered with a sheet of wrapping paper. Hold a crayon in each hand. Then with your arms comfortably extended (but not strained) draw two arcs on the paper, one with each hand. This gives your maximum working area. If you are cutting cookies, or doing desk work, or addressing Christmas cards, or wrapping packages, you can use this whole width. You can reach out to cut the dough, or you can place anywhere within it reference books or cards already written, or you can keep your balls of string and labels somewhere at the edge of this area. If you are of average height, this maximum depth will be about 20 inches, and your work counter need be no wider than this.

Again draw an arc with each hand, but with your elbow bent. The area inside these arcs is your normal working area. This is where you will do *most* of your work, whether it is chopping or beating or washing or typewriting or sewing. It will probably be about 16 inches deep. You should not have to reach beyond it in any job you do constantly, or for any tool you use a great deal.

The place where the two smaller arcs overlap is where both hands can work most comfortably together. So if you are mixing a cake and holding a bowl with one hand and a spoon with the other, you will keep them in this overlapping area. Place your tools and ingredients not beyond the place where the larger arcs overlap.

Most people do these things naturally, without thinking much about it. It is certainly natural to set a mixing bowl down in front of you and not off to one side where you have to stretch to reach it. Where we go astray is in not questioning the arrangements that we find ready-made, like the mass-produced dish closets and sinks and desks and chests of drawers.

A portable work place is a great help. This is your table on wheels. You can train yourself to push or pull it around with you wherever you go, like a faithful dog ready to fetch and carry. One lady actually named hers Fido.

Fido is especially helpful with the *get ready* and the *clean up*. He will carry clean dishes to the table and soiled ones to the sink. He will carry laundry or cleaning things or groceries to their final resting places, and you can load him with paint cans or serving things or party fixings. You can place trays on his shelves, each one set with a complete place setting for serving supper in the living room or outdoors. Use him for cleaning things, for pails or pans of water when you are washing floors or woodwork, for the vacuum cleaner and its attachments. The portable table can be 32 inches high, or whatever height you prefer for long-handled tools. This will save you the trouble of making pull-out boards or using the sink well.

Try to make use of the principle of the wheel wherever you can. Furniture that can roll is much easier to move. If possible put casters on heavy pieces. Put wheels on the end of your ironing board. Wheels can be mounted on your work chair. The best place for them is a few inches above the floor on the back legs, so the chair can be tilted and pushed around easily. You have wheels or runners on your vacuum cleaner. Use a wheelbarrow or a dolly to move outdoor furniture. Use your shopping cart wherever you can.

Another principle of physics that you can use is gravity. It is much easier to let things fall than to put them down. We discussed this previously under momentum. Of course, you shouldn't throw your china into the sink or hurl your cleaning basket down the stairs, though you might feel like it sometimes. But you can roll a bundle of laundry down the stairs. Perhaps you can have a laundry chute built in.

Gravity feed bins in the kitchen are good for flour or sugar. See if you can get them installed over your mix center. If not, get the sort of canister that can be tipped instead of lifted.

Some kitchens have a hole in the counter beside the sink so that vegetable peelings can be pushed across the counter to drop down into the garbage can below. The simplest use of gravity is the chopping board, on which the knife moves downward to cut the vegetables. If the chopped vegetables are then pushed off the board into the cooking pot, instead of being put in by handfuls, that is using gravity again. Of course, if they fall off on the floor, that's a little too much gravity. Set the pan in the sink, below the counter level.

Managers of big institutional kitchens, where vegetables are prepared in large quantities, go to a lot of trouble to get arrangements like these because the saving of time and energy and money amounts to quite a lot. You may not save much on one pound of beans. But consider how often in the next five years you are going to chop a pound of beans. It adds up.

Speaking of chopping beans, it is a good idea to *pre-position* a bean-slicer where you can simply take hold of a handle and go to work. There are a number of gadgets like this that can be pre-positioned—that is, set up where the hand can simply reach out and go to work with them. The commonest example is the wall can opener. The desk fountain pen is another. The coffee dispenser, the soap dispenser, the paper towel holder, the reference dictionary or cook book ready to use on its own little slanting shelf, are all examples of things pre-positioned in the work place.

Try to arrange your work place so *the hands don't have to do all the work*. The foot-pedal garbage pail has already been mentioned. There is also a foot-pedal refrigerator which lets you use both hands for carrying food. Invent other ways of using your feet. Put knobs or pulls on low drawers so you can slide them out with your toe. You operate the sewing machine switch or the vacuum cleaner switch with your foot. Try to rig up other switches that work the same way.

Holding devices are very handy in the work place. Industry constantly makes use of clamps and vises to hold the work in place while the hands manipulate it. You can use them too. The clamp that holds the meat grinder to the table is one. A vise or a clip can be used to hold papers together on a desk, or materials or patterns together on a sewing table. There is a gadget that holds the telephone receiver on your shoulder and leaves your hands free to knit or write while you talk. Suction cups hold the bowl of the mixer in place or the meat platter on the table. Papers can be impaled on a nail, or a roast on a cutting board by means of spikes. The simplest holding device is the little guard rail that keeps your grocery packages on the shelf. A tray with divisions to keep dishes from sliding around is another, and so is the rail around the top of your wheeled table, and the strap you use to keep the baby in the carriage. One mother rigged up a wheeled table with a small fence around the top edge, to use as a dressing table for her baby. This was a combination of two good work methods—the wheel and the holding device.

How is the light in your work place? Eye fatigue is the most insidious kind there is, and it is greatly increased by poor light. In the days before we could simulate daylight in our homes, people got up at dawn and went to bed when it was dark. There was not much else they could do except sit by the fire and tell stories, or go walking in the moonlight. Nowadays, we carry on our work no matter what time it is, but we don't always see to it that we have enough light. The amount of light needed for efficient seeing will be discussed in the chapter on working conditions.

Think of your home as a series of work centers. Look at each one and think of the things you do there, and ask yourself, "Is the work place arranged for the best possible work method? What can I do to cut down or combine operations, transportations, inspections? How can I eliminate delay?"

When you are doing jobs with the hands and fingers, think of the therbligs. Ask yourself, "What can I do so that one hand doesn't simply hold while the other works? How can I place things so I don't have to search? How can I cut down transport empty?"

Sometimes the work method tells you what your arrangement should be, and sometimes the arrangement of the work place dictates the method.

Chapter 6

Making Changes—Tools and Storage

As soon as you begin to think of your home as a series of work centers, you start planning how to store in each center the tools, supplies and equipment you need there. Then each work center becomes a storage center and you want to find the best ways of storing things. This may mean a simple rearrangement, like hanging a saucepan over the stove instead of putting it in a pot closet. Or it can turn into a major construction job, with new shelves and cupboards and counters.

Whatever changes you make now will depend on how much money, time and energy you want to spend. Your decision will depend first on how much you have to spend, and secondly on how much it is worth while spending.

If you are living in a rented house, for instance, you may not think it worth while to invest much money. With the use of some time and energy and a little money you can put up some new shelves. With no money at all you can switch things around to save yourself steps and labor. If you are staying a few weeks, it won't be worth while to do much. If you expect to stay for several years, more expensive improvements will pay off.

But before embarking on storage rearrangements it is a good idea to take a look at the things you are going to store. You want to examine them with a very objective eye, to decide whether they are *worth storing*.

Every home contains a larger or smaller collection of gadgets and gimcracks.

You buy something that appeals to you, or somebody brings you a present, or a salesman unloads some new invention on you, and the first thing you know, your house is full of *things*. You find yourself pushing three or four patent beaters out of the way before you find the old wooden stirring spoon you really want. You have five or six kinds of brushes when two would serve all your purposes. You have any number of odd cake tins, cooky cutters, unmatched cheese glasses and jars without lids.

So take a good look. Here is where you are going to have some fun if you are one of those who likes to throw things out. Here is where you will suffer if you are the kind that holds on to things.

It is a good idea to start in the kitchen because there are more tools here than anywhere else in the house (unless you happen to have an automobile mechanic in the family). The kitchen is important, too, because most homemakers spend a large proportion of their time there. It is estimated that the average woman spends a minimum of four hours a day in the kitchen merely working on meal preparation and clean-up. And of course the kitchen is the scene of many other activities. There is washing, ironing, dining and perhaps desk work. And many kitchens nowadays are being designed like the old-fashioned kitchen of colonial days, which was work room, playroom and sitting room all rolled into one.

The first thing for you to do is to get everything out and look at it. Open wide those cupboard doors and see if you really need everything that is behind them.

Here is what one family did before having their kitchen done over. The husband put a bushel basket in the middle of the floor. He then took every single thing out of the closets and off the shelves, and asked his wife when she had last used it.

If she said, "Oh, now, let's see, I haven't used that since Aunt Hattie came to dinner a year ago last Easter," he put it in the basket. If she said, "Oh, that! Why, I couldn't cook a meal without it!" he put it back where it belonged. The basket full of things that had not been used in a year was taken up to the attic.

"Whenever you want one of those things," he said, "you tell me and I will go and get it for you."

She never asked for one of them. If by chance she thought of one, she found she could use something else just as well.

This little story goes to show that many of the things you think you can't live without are forgotten as soon as they are out of sight.

So decide first: *are the tools you have really the ones you want?* If you don't use them, toss them out.

Decide how many bowls, vases, refrigerator dishes and jars you really could use if you used them all. One woman made a habit of saving all screw top jars because she might make jam some day and because they were handy for keeping left-over food. She had whole shelves full of empty jars gathering dust until a friend pointed out that she never made jam, and that if she stuffed the refrigerator with jars she wouldn't use more than two dozen.

Decide which dishes you really use and get rid of the rest. Decide what knives, spoons, choppers, slicers, beaters are really useful and keep those and no others. Get rid of that spatula whose handle is always coming off, that extra can opener which you are always picking up instead of the one that really works.

Of the tools you keep, decide: *are they the best of their kind that you can afford?*

This doesn't mean you must go on a buying spree. It doesn't mean you should toss out your old egg-beater and spend half a week's salary on an automatic mixer. It does mean that often a small and inexpensive tool is a worth-while purchase because it's a real labor-saver. So when you replace tools, buy carefully, knowing what you want them to do for you.

Consider what a tool is. It is an extension of yourself. It lengthens your reach. It does things your fingers can't do. It gives you added strength and power. So learn certain principles about tools.

First, a tool should be of suitable material, and of the best quality available, depending on the job it has to do. Stainless steel stirring spoons and pancake turners, for instance, are better than tin because they don't rust. But tin pie plates are better than stainless steel because they can be given a coating of grease so that food won't stick to them.

Knives should be of good quality so that they will take and keep a cutting edge, and a carborundum knife sharpener is better than the kind that is made of several little wheels.

Then a tool should be safe. A wall-type can opener, for example, is both better and safer than the old hand type for opening most cans. A sharp knife is safer than a dull one. Tools should have handles that will stay on, and should have no sharp projecting edges where they don't belong. Heat-resistant glass is safer than ordinary glass, though it splinters when broken. Good electric appliances are insulated so that the user can't get a shock.

Try to have *multi-purpose tools* whenever possible. You save time and space that way. A combination slicer and scraper, a combination can opener, bottle opener and lever for prying off lids is more efficient than a separate tool for each purpose. It takes up less room, and you don't have to lay one thing down and pick up another.

Try to have tools that cut down the *get ready* and the *clean-up.* If a special tool is used for only a very small job, the work of getting it out, washing and putting it away may take longer than using a tool already at hand. For instance, if a recipe says to use a quarter of a cup of chopped nuts, you might use the food grinder. On the other hand, you might say, "I'll have to wash it because it's dusty, then I'll wash it again after I use it, and that's a nuisance because of all the little holes that get filled up with food. I'll just cut up the nuts with a knife and be done with it."

If you find you never use the food grinder for these reasons, you had better give it away, or at least put it where it won't collect dust and get in the way.

Some tools have handles that are hard to hold—a stirring spoon may have a sharp handle that cuts into your hand, or one that gets too hot to grasp. Discard it for one with a rounded, heat-resistant handle.

Studies have been made in industry to find out what is the best kind of handle for a crank or a screwdriver, with which work is done, or for a pail, where the hand carries a load. It has been shown that the best handle is one that comes in contact with the largest amount of hand surface. Thus a tool like a stirring spoon or a fork for lifting a joint of meat should have a thick, cylindrical handle.

Try to get tools with devices that free your hands for other work—foot pedals and switches. Garbage pails and sewing machines are made with foot pedals. Vacuum cleaners have a button that you step on to switch them on or off. The doctor's lavatory has a foot pedal to turn the water on and off, and many a housewife could make good use of this convenience.

A box or hamper for rags or laundry frees your hands by the simple fact that it will stand up by itself, whereas a bag has to be held with one hand while being filled with the other.

Some tools can be used with one hand instead of two—certain kinds of beaters, or the one-handled flour sifter, or a grater fixed in place on a board. A mixing bowl with a suction base will stay put while you beat eggs with one hand.

Have duplicates of inexpensive tools at the different centers where you work. You might have measuring spoons, cups, paring knives and stirring spoons at the range, and another set at the mix center, unless the two centers are adjacent.

Have extra containers for staples at the places where you need small quantities of them. A flour-shaker near the stove saves the trouble of pulling the lid off the canister. Extra salt and pepper shakers and sugar bowls at the range and mix centers save steps.

Canisters which are easy to open and close and are clearly labeled save lots of time and temper.

Tools that save you the trouble of frequent inspection are worth having. Meat and candy thermometers, for instance, make unnecessary the less accurate methods of poking, smelling, and dropping into cold water. Accurate measurements save the trouble of tasting (though many cooks would say that the old-fashioned methods can't be dispensed with altogether, and a tasting machine has not yet been invented). A coffee pot with markings for water and coffee will save the trouble of measuring.

Thermostats for temperature control save inspection on toasters, ovens, irons, refrigerators and percolators. Speed controls do the same with your food mixer and electric fan.

If your oven has no thermostat, you can improvise one. Use an oven thermometer and observe where the gas cock is when the temperature is 300, 400, 500, and so on. Then make a mark at that point on the stove enamel in indelible ink.

Try to have:

Pans and lids with heat-resistant handles.
Pans whose capacity you know.
Lids that fit pans.
Tools that save your fingers and extend your grasp—tongs and long-handled forks.
Dishes that can be used for cooking, serving and storage.
Trays for carrying a number of things at once.
Wheeled tables for toting still more things at once.
Mops that don't need wringing.
Dustpans and brushes with long handles to save stooping and breathing in dust.
Tools that are easy to clean—colanders rather than wire strainers; a beater that can be dunked in the dishpan rather than one with ball bearings that mustn't be wet; containers with round inside corners; pots made of smooth, chip-proof material with no unreachable corners to collect grease.
Tools that can stand hot water—steel instead of plastic.

Tools that are unbreakable—plastic or metal rather than china or glass.

Tools that don't need polishing—steel or china instead of tin, glass instead of agate or iron.

Tools that come apart easily if they're meant to (slicers and grinders) and that stay together if they're meant to do that (handles riveted on rather than cemented on).

Utensils that fit together well for easy storage—square refrigerator dishes instead of bowls.

Tools and cloths with loops and rings for easy hanging.

Dusting mitts instead of rags.

A shopping cart that can be used for groceries, laundry and other transportation jobs.

A basket to hold brushes, cloths, bottles of polish, containers into which to empty ashtrays, and other cleaning equipment, to be carried along when you clean house. Two such if you have a two-story house. Try to get one which fits your shopping cart, or use your portable table, to wheel it around, as well as to carry your vacuum cleaner attachments.

An ironing board with wheels at one end, and a cover fastened on by lacings instead of tacks.

Racks for clothes.

Electric cords with switches in the plugs, so they don't have to be pulled out and pushed in all the time.

An electric mixer, or at least a smoothly working beater with a large handle for easy holding.

A comfortable work chair.

Scissors of various sizes.

A simple kit of good carpenter's tools.

A vacuum cleaner which is simple to get ready and put away.

Plastic sponges, aluminum foil, paper dusters and towels, paper bags for waste disposal, throw-away dishes and ashtrays, and the various new kinds of furniture polishes, cleansers, glass cleaners, floor waxes and hand cleaners that reduce work and make the necessary work easier.

One more piece of advice about something that can't be classified as a tool, but is certainly part of your equipment. Take the trouble to have comfortable work clothing and, what is just as important, be sure what you wear is *right*. It's a bad work method to use up your old afternoon dresses and high-heeled shoes "around the house." In the first place, they are apt to be tight and awkward, and in the second, they don't express a proper respect for the job. If you were hiring someone to help you with your work, you would expect her to wear suitable work clothes, so it's up to you to do the same.

There are all sorts of attractive work clothes—pinafores, aprons with big pockets, dresses that open out flat for easy ironing, slacks and shirts in lovely colors, and comfortable shoes that look nice and make you want to bounce around the house. So here's a good excuse to go shopping.

Now having decided what things you want to keep in your house, you must decide where to store them. The modern tendency is to streamline everything so that the result is like a picture in a magazine, with everything under cover.

You should do this if you like it. Some people don't like their tools and supplies exposed to view. They say it is distracting to the eye, and dust-collecting. If this is how you feel, do everything you can to have cupboards with doors that close, and plenty of drawer space for your utensils.

But if you haven't the cupboards and can't afford them, don't feel too badly. The open shelf system has its advantages too. First of all, the streamlined kitchen only looks like a picture when everything is put away. If the coffee pot is left out or a few dishes are left to drain, the room looks messy. Rooms that are lived in and used should be functional, and that means that if your egg-beater shows, it's right where you can seize it and get to work in one motion.

Now, how to place your things most effectively.

The guiding rule is: store the things you use most often in the most convenient positions.

a. At the place where you will use them first.
b. Where you don't have to bend or stretch, or move something else out of the way to get them or put them back.

In your kitchen you may always have stored your pots and pans and baking dishes in the pan cupboard, your groceries in the food cupboard, your dishes and glassware in the dish closet, and your knives, stirring spoons and other utensils in the drawers of your kitchen cabinet.

For some things you may have to climb on a stool because the dish closet shelves are high. If you want the large platter you must lift a lot of small ones off it. For the Dutch oven you must get down on your knees, and for the grapefruit knife perhaps you rummage in a drawer. To get supplies for cooking you have to walk back and forth because some of them are used first at the counter where you mix things, others at the sink where you soak them in water, others, like coffee or oatmeal, directly at the stove.

You saw in the coffee-making motion study how a slight change in the storage places of coffee, saucepan and coffee pot saved time and energy. Experts have made time and motion studies to show that you can really make your shelves and drawers work for you by saving you steps.

Instead of classifying things according to what they are—pans, dishes, groceries—classify them according to where you use them.

Most saucepans, for instance, are used first at the sink because you put water in them before placing them on the stove. See if you can arrange shelves over the sink, or a hanging panel near it, or a cupboard over it, or between the sink and the stove. Here you can store some of your pans, your strainers, brushes and knives for cleaning vegetables, measuring cups, dishwashing utensils, soaps and cleansers. At the sink too you accumulate vegetable parings and dish scrapings, so the garbage can should be kept near by.

Small tools can be hung on hooks, or in slotted racks, or by means of two nails driven close together.

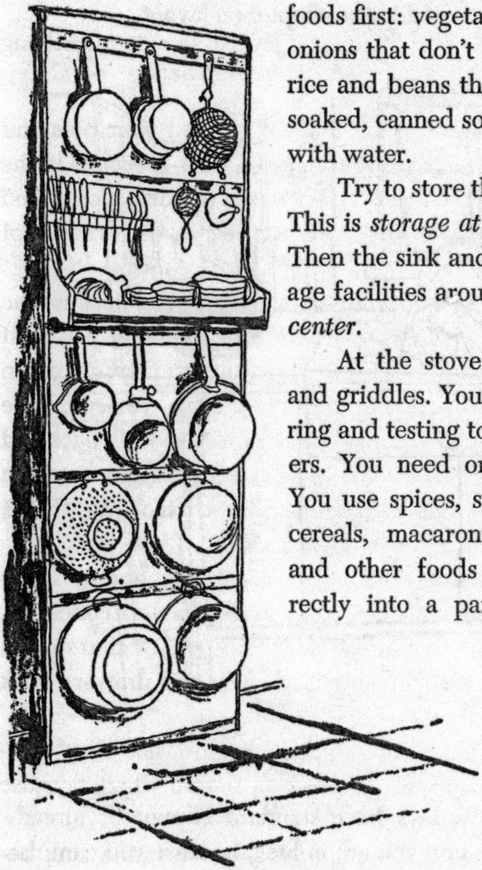

At the sink too you handle certain foods first: vegetables like potatoes and onions that don't belong in the ice box, rice and beans that must be washed or soaked, canned soups which are diluted with water.

Try to store these things at the sink. This is *storage at the point of first use.* Then the sink and the shelves and storage facilities around it become the *sink center.*

At the stove you use frying pans and griddles. You use lids. You use stirring and testing tools and pancake turners. You need one or two saucepans. You use spices, salt, sugar, tea, coffee, cereals, macaroni, canned vegetables and other foods which you pour directly into a pan on the stove. You need a can opener. There should also be adequate working surface. Then you have a *stove center.*

When you mix cookies and meat loaves, make a pie or cookies, or put together a pudding or a salad, you work at a counter. This should be your *mix center.* Here you need measuring tools, rolling pin, bowls, stirring spoons. You need supplies such as flour, sugar, salt, baking powder, prepared mixes, seasonings, oil, vinegar.

Some of these things are used at the stove too. If your stove and mix center happen to be close together, you can arrange shelves that will serve both. There are also advantages in having sink and stove close together, with a counter between. These arrangements will be discussed in the chapter on layout.

Most kitchens nowadays have standard cupboards already installed. If yours does not, you are in luck, because you can plan the shelves that will best fill your individual needs.

By looking at the things you need to store, you will see what kind of shelves to store them on. It has been found that shallow shelves, on which you place utensils or packages one layer deep, are best. For instance, shelves for canned goods or boxes of rice or beans or pancake flour should be from four to six inches deep. You can put very shallow racks two or three inches deep on the inside of cupboard doors to hold spices and small packages of foods.

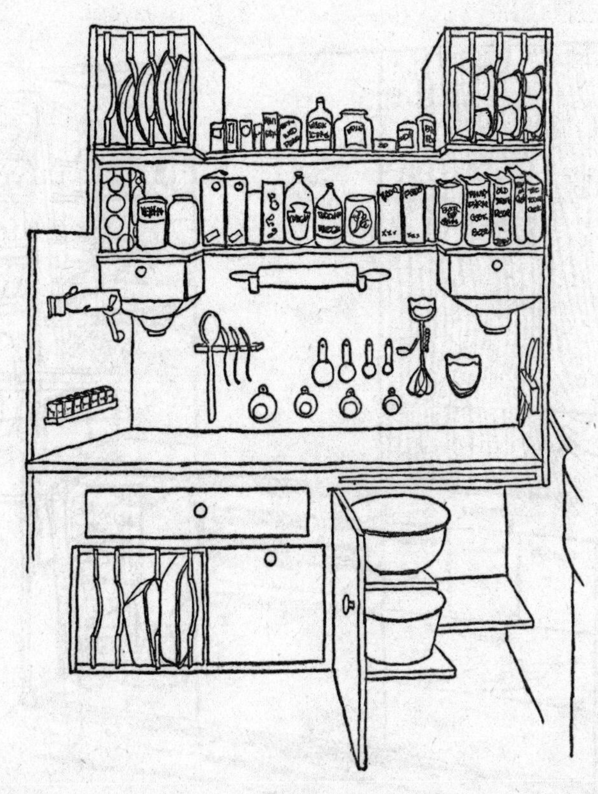

If your grocery shelves are deeper than six inches, don't store the supplies more than one layer deep, unless the second layer is the same as the first. That is, you can put a can of tomatoes behind another can of tomatoes, but not behind a can of milk. Thus you will be able to see all your supplies at a glance, and you will never have to lift out one object to get at another. This is called *one-motion storage.*

If you decide to build shelves to hold pots and bowls, don't make them more than eighteen inches deep. Actually most pans will fit very nicely on a twelve-inch shelf, and as this is the width of the ordinary pine board, you won't need to do any rip-saw work.

Three- and four-inch shelves are very handy to hold small utensils like measuring cups, little pitchers, orange squeezers, and the like.

Everyday dishes should be stored in stacks of their own kind. Never put small saucers on top of big ones, or small bowls inside of larger bowls, if you can help it. Build your shelves close together and store your serving bowls and platters one layer deep. Then, when you want the blue pottery bowl for the potatoes, you just lift the blue pottery bowl off the shelf, and not a whole nest of bowls.

Don't put cups on hooks. Set them on the shelves in twos. Don't nest glasses. Set them in rows on the shelves. The rows may be two or three layers deep, provided the layers are all of the same kind. But don't put goblets behind tumblers because you will have to move the tumblers before you can get at the goblets.

The less you handle your dishes the smaller the chance of breakage, and the less strain there will be on your back, arms and shoulders.

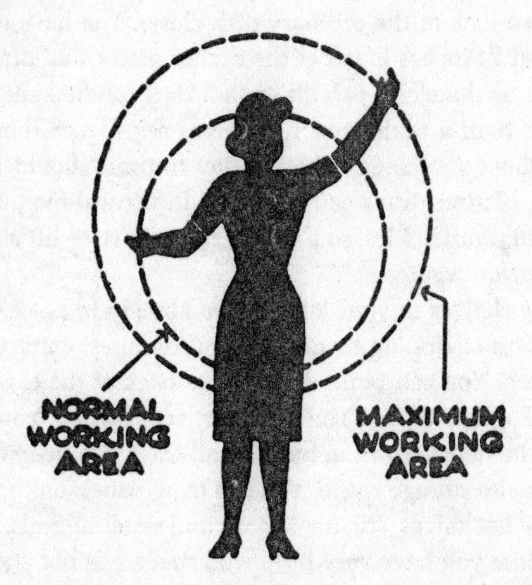

Here is the best way to decide how high or low your things should be stored: don't have anything that you use frequently on a shelf higher or lower than you can reach comfortably without stretching or stooping.

Stand about a foot back from the wall. Swing your arms from the shoulder to make the widest circle you can on the wall. If you are of average height, the top of the circle will be about 72 inches from the floor. The bottom will be about 25 inches from the floor. Therefore don't put anything you use often on a shelf higher than 72 or lower than 25 inches from the floor, if you can avoid it.

Now make another circle by moving your arm from the elbow. This is the circle of greatest use to you. The things you use not only often, but constantly, should be stored within this circle. The salt, the paring knife, the can opener, the soap should be where you can just put out your hand and touch them.

The things you use seldom, like flower vases and the birthday cake plate, or the big roasting pan, can be put either higher or lower than your comfortable reach.

Take a look at the ordinary dish closet. You have to lift your arms about 24 inches to get at the dinner plates, and dinner plates are heavy. If the closet is built so that they can be kept on a shelf no higher than a table, and no shelves are higher than you can reach without stretching, what a relief to those shoulder muscles!

Pans, platters, trays can be stored in vertical files, or on door racks, or in slanting files, so that you never have to lift a pile to get at the one you want.

If the shelves in your kitchen are already in place, what can you do, short of ripping them out? You can insert extra shelves between them. You can build steps at the back of the closet to hold small packages or dishes. You can insert vertical files. You can build racks on the doors. You can build small trays into deep drawers to give you more storage space. You can hang panels on the available wall space for knives, stirring spoons and small utensils.

Suppose you have very little wall space and not enough shelf space. You can build cabinets hinged to the wall panels, opening out to give you twice or three times as much shelf space as would be supplied by one wall cabinet alone.

Store the heaviest things, like the flour and cereal and sugar and the big mixing bowls, at table height, and the light things higher if necessary.

There is usually some place in the kitchen for eating. In fact, more and more kitchens are being planned as centers for all sorts of family activities—eating, resting, entertaining, hobbies.

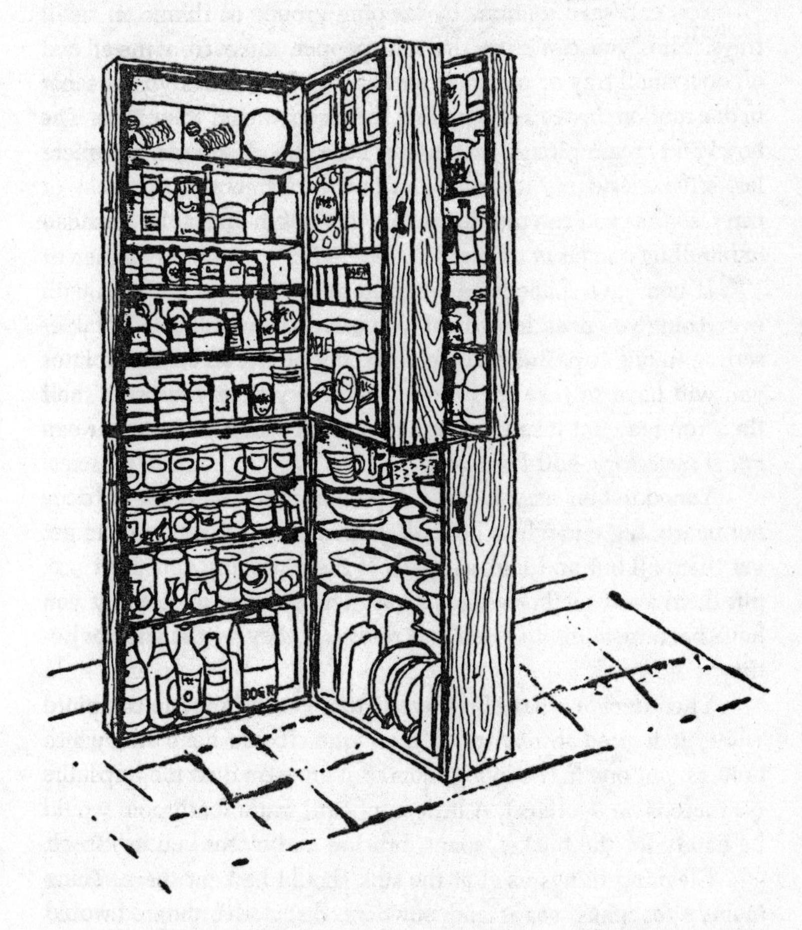

The eating center should be out of the main flow of traffic. Near it you should have the dishes you use every day, as well as the foods that are served directly without cooking, such as dry cereals, cookies, spreads, condiments, crackers, as well as napkins, mats, hot pads and silver. On a shelf near by should be the toaster, the waffle iron and other electric pieces used at the table. Then you can set the table with a minimum of walking back and forth.

You can save motions by keeping groups of things on small trays. Thus you can store the salt, pepper, mustard, vinegar and oil on a small tray or rack on a shelf, and take them all to the table in one motion, instead of handling them separately. Keep the sugar bowl and cream pitcher on another little tray. Keep cheeses, pickles, olives, leftovers in small jars in the refrigerator on racks or trays, so that you can pull the whole tray out in one motion instead of handling one jar at a time.

If you have space for a wheeled table that can be piled with everything you need for a meal, you can do the whole job of table-setting in one trip. But don't let anything be stored on top of it, or you will have to take these things off every time you use it, and then you may not take the trouble to use it. Put a sign on it: *Keep off!* If necessary, add *Positively!*

Your kitchen may include a broom closet. This is probably not nearly big enough to hold *all* your cleaning things. As before, get them all out and look at them. If there are any you don't use, put them away or throw them away. Throw away all the rags you have been meaning to wash and re-use. If they're stiff with polish they're no good.

Then decide what else there is that can be kept in the place where it is used instead of in the closet. If you have two whisk brooms, put one in the living room. Put an extra dust mop upstairs (if there is an upstairs). A little cupboard in the bathroom would be handy for the bucket, soaps, brushes and cloths you use there.

Cleaning things used at the sink should be kept there. These include dishpans, soaps and powders, dishcloths, mops, brushes and scrapers. Build a cupboard under the sink to hold a scrub pail, cleaning supplies and floor cloths, or have a cabinet beside the sink to hold dishwashing equipment plus the utensils which belong at the sink center.

Something for quick tidying should be kept in other rooms—cloth or paper dusters or tissues in a drawer in the living room and in the bedroom for wiping up ashes or spilled liquids; a waste paper basket in each room.

Then for the things that remain to be kept in the cleaning closet, see that your closet is adequate. You may keep in it a broom, dust mop, dustpan and brush, carpet sweeper; perhaps the vacuum cleaner, a wet mop and a wall brush. There will be boxes and bottles of waxes, polish, soap, cleaning fluid and detergents. Put them all together in a corner of the kitchen and look at them. The carpet sweeper's box is usually 14 by 10 inches. The mop end of a wet or dust mop is about 9 inches wide. Handles of brooms and mops are from 54 to 61 inches long. Use these dimensions in figuring the size of your closet. It has to be high enough and wide enough and deep enough to take all these things without crowding. Design it so you don't have to take out four or five tools to get at the carpet sweeper. A wide shallow closet where implements are stored one layer deep, with shelves at the side for boxes and bottles, is best. If you can't enlarge your closet or haven't space for a regular one, fasten a wooden panel against the wall with hooks and clips for your tools. If they are hung flat against the wall they can't get bunched together.

The living room is another place where many activities go on, especially in small homes. It is used for rest, for play, for listening to radio and watching television. This is where Johnny and his fellow cowboys ambush cattle rustlers, where Mother does her sewing, where Father balances the check book, where Grandpa plays checkers with Mary, and where guests are entertained.

Not only must the room be attractive and orderly, but there must be a place for all the things that are needed here, and a quick way to clean up after use.

For rest, there must be comfortable chairs with a good light for each one. There must be shelves and low tables for books and ash trays. For entertaining or watching television, folding or nested tables and hassocks or folding chairs are good.

Now look at all the things that are kept in the living room. If the children play here, their toys and books may be left lying around. Perhaps a chest or a drawer or a good-looking box could hold certain toys that are often used here. It will be easier for the children to put them away if they don't have to carry them too far. A wagon or a big truck can be used to load blocks and little cars for garaging. For the youngest ones, a blanket spread on the floor will stake out their claim and keep them from overrunning the whole room.

If you do your sewing here, a small cabinet for supplies, a comfortable chair, a good light and a small table placed in a convenient corner will reduce the *get ready* and *clean up* and make it unnecessary for you to bring your sewing materials from the bedroom and carry them back there every time you sit down to work. Of course if you do a great deal of sewing, a storage unit elsewhere in the house would be more practical. It can be a complete closet, with built-in drawers, space for the machine, shelves, and a place to hang garments and store the dress form and ironing board.

The desk in the living room is often a shambles because the family often uses it to dump everything they can't classify. A desk is a work place which should be treated respectfully. It should have a good light. It should contain a calendar, pencil sharpener, pencils, ink, pen, paper clips, rubber bands, scissors, stationery, stamps, blotters and small memo pads. A desk with pigeon holes is best, but if you can't have that, divide the drawers with strips of wood or cardboard so your supplies will stay where they belong. Divide the deepest drawer with supports so that file folders for your important papers will stand upright.

For entertaining, it is well to have coasters and napkins where they are easily reached. A decorative box on the bookcase or the lower shelf of the coffee table can hold them.

In addition to these needed articles, the living room usually holds a great many things which cannot be thought of as tools, because one does not work with them. However, we use them, and work is required to keep them in order. These are the books and magazines, the bric-a-brac, the fancy dishes and boxes and cigarette lighters, the record albums and sheet music, and all the other things which an active family collects and leaves lying around the house.

They should be examined and weeded out. This ought to be a project for the whole family, because if one person undertakes to send or throw anything away, the other members are sure to come down on him or her like a ton of bricks.

Somewhere in your living room you may have a catch-all—a drawer or box or a glass bowl, or the desk above mentioned, where all kinds of objects are tossed: paper clips, letters, safety pins, candle ends, money order stubs, sales checks, hairpins, the button off Grandpa's vest, pencils, half a stick of chewing gum—things you don't want to throw away but for which there is no proper place. In a way this is handy, because you always know where to find a pencil or a paper clip (unless someone has just taken the last one and forgotten to put it back). In another sense it's a menace. It looks awful and there is no system to it. If you really need those money order stubs and sales checks, ten to one they won't be there when you go to look for them.

Actually, everything in this catch-all can be classified. Take the things out one at a time, no matter how small they are. Put the clips in one pile, the pins in another, the buttons in a third. Have a box for each category. Have a box for unanswered letters. Have a folder for unpaid bills, a big clip or envelope for sales checks and receipts, a jar for pencils. This is the principle used in office filing systems—a separate folder for each subject.

Apply this principle to everything you have and you will soon bring order out of the greatest chaos.

Now that you have done the weeding out, for a place to file the things you want to keep in the living room a storage wall can't be beat. Built along one end of a room, or as a partition between two rooms, it is both decorative and practical. It can be as cheap or as expensive as you like. It can be made of planks laid on bricks, with a curtain hung across the front, or it can be a handsome cabinet job.

The best kind is of course the most flexible. A wall made of standard-sized cabinets of various types can be taken apart and put together in different ways or in different parts of the house. The cabinets can be shelves and chests of drawers and cupboards to hold books, records, games and music. There can be a niche for the radio and record player, a desk, a place for card tables and chairs. It can even hold the vacuum cleaner if the living room is where that is principally used. Make your shelves and cupboards no deeper than the largest thing to be stored in them. Usually 24 inches will be deep enough for cupboards, and 12 inches for bookshelves. Adjustable shelves and shallow drawers are best for making the most use of space.

The Small Homes Council of the University of Illinois has developed a number of designs for storage units, with dimensions based on a standard unit of measurement called a module. The module is 4 inches long, and all their designs are made in multiples of 4 inches. This makes for economy in cutting materials, and also for ease in fitting the parts together. The basic storage units can be assembled side by side, back to back, or stacked one above another.*

Most of these suggestions emphasize the wisdom of storing at the point of first use, so far as possible, and depending on the kind of house you have. Of course you won't store the vacuum cleaner in the living room if you have a large and formal house, but in a small house, where space is a problem, this might be a good solution. Also, you have to use common sense. You don't keep the bottle of furniture polish on the living room table just because this is where you first use it.

Think of storage problems in two ways: first, in relation to the room or the part of the house you are reorganizing; and second, in relation to the things you are storing and the activities that center around these things.

Take the matter of clothing. You might say that clothing is usually kept in people's bedrooms because that is where they dress, and that is where they have their closets and chests of drawers.

* Household Storage Units, Small Homes Council Bulletin No. C 51, University of Illinois, Urbana, Ill.

But examine your family's habits. Is all dressing done in the bedrooms? No.

The baby, for instance, is often dressed in the bathroom where you bathe him. If there is space, a little chest or some shelves can hold shirts, diapers and other things that are often changed. Or if you wash the baby or the small children in the kitchen, keep one drawer there for their clothes, soap, cotton and other supplies. This becomes a washing and dressing center for small children.

Suppose you live in a studio apartment with a couch in the living room and a closet in the foyer. Storage may be a problem. You may have a handsome chest in the living room, using the top for a sideboard and the drawers for clothing. You may find yourself gathering up garments, accessories and cosmetics from hall and living room and rushing with them to do your dressing in the bathroom. It would be better in this case to try to get a small chest into the bathroom, to hang a shoebag on the bathroom door, and to keep your cosmetics on a small tray in the medicine closet or on top of the chest.

One couple had two rooms, a living room and a small bedroom which was not big enough for both beds and chests. They converted it into a dressing room by building in an extra closet, with shelves, mirror and sliding doors, and put studio beds in the living room.

A row of shelves built along the side of a closet can often take the place of bureau drawers and save space in the room. And shallow shelves or sliding trays give better storage for piles of shirts and underwear than deep wide drawers in which large piles of things get rumpled and small things get lost.

Try to keep all types of clothing together. This doesn't mean all shoes in one place, all dresses in another, and so on. It means keeping the clothes you need for work—dresses, shoes, hats—stored close to each other where you can get them quickly. Things you need less often—evening clothes, sportswear—can be stored in the less accessible places, farther back in the closet or on the higher shelves. You save time and motion in getting what you want, and you preserve your delicate dresses and sweaters from much handling.

Outdoor clothes can be kept in closets near the exits of a house. If your front hall has no closet, maybe you can make one with a rod and a shelf over it, and a good-looking curtain hung in front. This is a good place for guests' coats. Have a mirror near by. A shoe bag on the inside of a closet door is a good place for mittens, rubbers, clothes brushes and woolen hats. A towel rod is fine for scarves and ties, and a bar with snap clothespins attached is a good place to keep the family gloves. A small shelf with a guard rail fastened to the door is useful for jars of hand lotion, a clothes brush, or whatever you want just before going out.

The children need dressing centers of their own with low rods for hanging clothes, low drawers that slide in and out easily, and shelves for their hats and shoes. Closets and chests can be built out of orange crates if necessary, with drawers made of cheese boxes, the crates being piled up vertically or horizontally and painted or covered with oilcloth or paper.*

Keep shoes off the floor, so they won't be kicked around, and also to make house-cleaning easier. Keep hats on racks or in boxes, and put away those you don't use.

Closet doors supply extra space for holding things. You can build racks, shelves or even swinging panels on the inside and outside of your doors. The best kind of closet door, of course, is that which opens to expose the whole closet. The kind that is just an opening in a wall leaves a lot of storage space inaccessible. However, if your rooms are small you will gain floor space by removing the doors and hanging curtains or sliding or folding doors.

Architects and decorators have given much thought in recent

* Ella M. Cushman, Centers for Your Work and Leisure, Cornell Extension Bulletin 811, New York State College of Home Economics, Ithaca, New York.

years to the subject of storage places. Since housing has become so scarce and building so expensive, and domestic help so hard to find, we have had to squeeze ourselves and our belongings into smaller places and it takes a lot of squeezing.

Built-in storage is one of the answers. Closets and drawers can be fitted into many corners where conventional furniture wouldn't go. They can be planned to utilize space near the floor (under seats or work surfaces) or up near the ceiling. There is lots of good space going to waste up there.

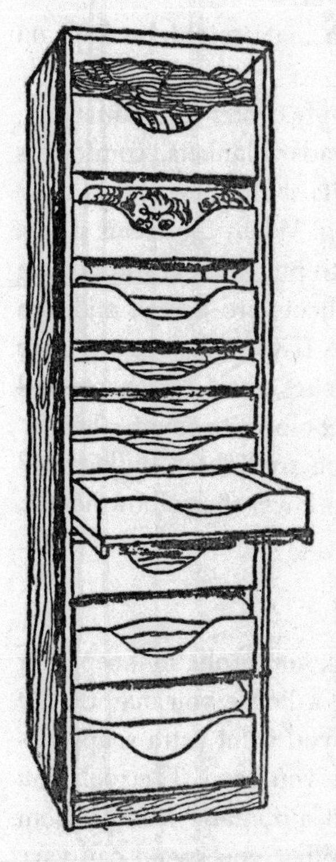

Built-in furniture lasts a long time because it isn't moved about or banged up, and it makes cleaning easy because you don't have to dust behind or under it. You must consider, though, how long you are going to live in the house. One family was so sold on built-ins that they had their house filled with them, and then came the day when they had to move. Lo and behold, they had almost no furniture for their new home. So plan your built-ins so that they will come out if necessary.

At every season there will be some clothing that is out of use. It ought to be put away where it will be kept clean and mothproof, and where you won't have to push it around to get at the things you want. Have garment bags at the back of closets, shelves up near the ceiling, special chests of drawers for these out-of-season clothes. Of course the very best arrangement is a special closet with a snug-fitting door, which you can use for nothing else but mothproof storage.

Linens

Linens are traditionally kept in a linen closet. This is all very well, and a pleasure to see, but it is also very convenient to separate the different kinds of linens and keep them nearer to the point of first use. A chest near the dining area is a better place than the hall linen closet for table linens, especially if you can get one with sliding trays, each big enough to hold one cloth with napkins, or one set of mats. Kitchen linens, dish towels, hand towels, pot holders, dish cloths, belong in a kitchen drawer.

Bath towels, wash cloths and bath mats might be kept on shelves in the bathroom.

Then the linen closet becomes a supply center for bedmaking, with places for sheets, pillow cases, pads, blankets, comforters and pillows. The ideal linen closet has its shelves for sheets close enough together to avoid much stacking. When the clean sheets come back from the laundry you'd like to put them at the bottom of a pile rather than on top. Piles of sheets are heavy, and you don't want to lift too large a pile at once. If your shelves are 15 to 18 inches deep, have them about 10 inches apart for sheets and pillow cases, and have the sheet shelves at elbow to counter height. Shelves for pillows and comforters, which are lighter, bulkier and less frequently changed, may be higher or lower than elbow height, and farther apart.

Laundry

If the laundry is done in the kitchen, you probably keep your supplies at the sink center. If you have a house you may do the laundry in the basement, in which case you want extra soaps, detergents, blue, starch, and whatever else you need. The tools you use vary from a washboard to the latest automatic washer, from an ordinary iron to an electric ironer. What you spend can vary from a dollar and a half to several hundred dollars. You have to decide whether the investment of much money will pay off within a reasonable time. If you have a great deal of laundry, and spend four or five dollars a week on it, the home laundry may pay for itself within a year or two. But if you spend only a dollar a week, the home laundry may not pay for itself in four or five years. However, if your time and energy are valuable, it may pay in savings of those two important resources.

Since many of the tools used in this department are large and stationary, the placing of them comes under the head of layout, which will be discussed in another chapter.

Hobbies and Games

These require space, and so do tools for household repairs. If you have a cellar or an extra room which can be turned into a combination workshop and game room, you are lucky. You can have racks for bats and tennis rackets and hockey sticks; shelves for skates, baseball gloves, flat games; drawers for small games like checkers and chess and cards, and a work bench along one wall with all your nails and screws in mayonnaise jars on narrow shelves above, and tools suspended by nails or hooks on a sheet of plywood. To be sure each tool is always put back where it belongs, draw its outline on the plywood. Have racks for different sizes of lumber and narrow shelves for tools like planes that can't be hung up. The workshop is like the laundry. You can go in for power tools and spend lots of money if you have it, and if you have the space.

But in a cellarless house or a small apartment the question of space is serious. You can put racks and shelves in the closets, and a work bench across one wall of a bedroom, but first consider carefully how many of these things you will really use. Remember that if they are too hard to get at, you won't be tempted to use them so often. This is a matter of standards. The fact that you haven't enough space for equipment may change your way of life. If you decide that the hobbies, the arts and crafts are too important to give up, you must manage somehow to get enough space to pursue them, and this may mean either that you get enough money to afford a bigger house on a more expensive level, or that you lower your standards and get a house which is bigger but cheaper because it's shabby or is in a less fancy neighborhood. Remember, man does not live by modern plumbing and picture windows alone.

Children's toys ought to get special mention here. They are perhaps the subject of more argument than any other household articles. First we buy them to give our offspring pleasure, and then we make their lives miserable by insisting that the toys be picked up and put away. Or they make our lives miserable by refusing to do so.

Children *like* to have their possessions scattered around like pebbles on a beach. At any rate, it isn't worth the cost to them to put their things away. If you want to teach them neatness, which is after all an adult virtue, you must make it pleasant for them. First, you must feel respectful toward their things, and not consider toys and all the odds and ends that children collect as so much junk to be shoved out of sight.

Then you must forget all the pretty pictures you ever saw in decorators' magazines, that is, if your child is over three and you really want him to use his room. These pictures show delightfully tidy shelves, with a few blocks here, a teddy bear there, and a row of beautiful books, all the same size and not at all dog-eared. Actually you know that your child's possessions consist of a mess of battered airplanes, trucks, trains, spools, crippled animals and mutilated dolls, a pile of dog-eared books of all sizes, large and small, an arsenal of guns, some crayons, pencils, papers, comic books, balls, and all kinds of games, each of which has about fifty-seven parts which are always getting mixed up and lost.

You can be determined about discarding things you haven't used in months, but *your child* can't. He loves them and can't give them up until he has outgrown them. A good way to store all this stuff is to build a counter along one end of his room, with shelves and drawers underneath. The counter will serve as a desk and workbench, the shelves will hold books and games, and the drawers are good for all the small bits and pieces that only your child can accumulate. Make the counter of plain unpainted wood so that he can really hammer and plane. Leave space underneath for a hangar or garage for his trucks or planes, so that they don't have to be picked up off the floor but can just be wheeled in and the doors closed after them.

If your child is older, and has reached the homework and letter-writing stage, there is nothing to equal an old-fashioned roll-top desk with pigeonholes to keep his clutter contained. If you can't find such a desk (and they're getting rare), build a row of pigeonholes over the desk or counter. Show him how to classify his belongings, give him a jar for pencils and buy him an old type-writer to peck at, and if he feels he has an office of his own, he *may* want to keep it in order.

Miscellaneous

This is that large category that includes old letters, seldom-worn hats, Christmas tree ornaments, books no longer read, pieces of material left over from dressmaking, odd bits of wood and wire, old road maps—all the things you have put away because they may come in handy, put away so haphazardly that when you might have a use for them you don't even know where they are. Things like these should be put in a basket, like the one mentioned at the beginning of this chapter, taken to the attic, and discarded at the end of a year. If you have no attic, you had better discard them at once, unless you can classify them and store them in clearly labeled boxes or drawers.

But perhaps it would be better not to use the phrase "at once." It takes time to reorganize storage places in a household. You cannot possibly do it all at once. However, as you go along, noticing how you walk from one end of the house to the other with towels, or with dishes, or with needle and thread, you will get ideas. Why shouldn't you keep the towels in the bathroom, the dishes on a shelf right beside the dinette table, the sewing things near the ironing board so you can mend as you iron?

Gradually you will see your house as a series of work centers, each containing whatever is needed for the activity it serves. Don't worry about spoiling the beauty of your home. The truly functional is beautiful too, for the simple reason that it doesn't get messed up.

And as good arrangements help to relieve tension and pressure, you will find an atmosphere of peace and serenity in the house that is more beautiful than anything else.

Chapter 7

Making Changes—Layout

Now that you know some of the main principles of scientific management, you can stand off and take a bird's-eye view of your house and see whether it is laid out in accordance with them.

Ideally, the layout of the house should come first, because you must have your rooms before you can set up your work places. This is really a matter for you and your architect to solve between you. It is a matter of the relation of the rooms and activity centers to each other. The architect should think of the house as a series of centers. We have been talking about work centers, but a house is more than that. There must be work, play and rest places in it. It should be planned so that it is easy to go from one center to another, from kitchen to living room, from living room to bedrooms, from bedrooms to bath, and so on, without getting in the way of anybody who is using the rooms, and without making unnecessary steps or detours. There must be enough space at each center for storage for the things to be used there. Good layout should consider the personalities and habits of the people who live in the house, and should place the most used centers in the most convenient places, as tools that are used constantly are stored within elbow reach.

Of course if you're building a home and money is no object, you can have it custom-tailored to suit your family as you would have a suit made to order. Even if you have to economize, you have a good deal of leeway in a house that is built just for you. At least you can choose what you will do without, and of the space you can afford, pick the most useful.

Possibly you can make use of the unit construction developed by the Small Homes Council of the University of Illinois, whose storage units we have mentioned before. Separate rooms or groups of rooms are designed as standard units, with standard measurements, so that they can be combined in different ways depending on the needs of the family and on the building site. There is a unit consisting of bedroom, bath and dressing facilities. Others are made up of living and dining areas. There are work units consisting of kitchen, laundry, utility room and eating place, and others containing garage with work space, or extra rooms to be used as separate living room, bedroom, study, porch or playroom.*

The dimensions are all multiples of four inches—the basic unit of measurement, called a module—so that they will fit together nicely, and a family can start with one or two rooms and add more whenever they like.

But suppose you're not building a house according to your own plans, but taking over a house or apartment built for some "average" family of today or twenty years ago. You've got to fit your family and their activities into it. This means making some changes, and it also means you have to consider again what you want to spend in the way of money, time and energy. You can spend little or nothing, you can spend a moderate amount, or you can toss your whole bankroll into the place.

* *Contemporary Houses Developed from Room Units,* Small Homes Council, University of Illinois, Urbana, Ill.

Fashions change. In colonial days the kitchen was the living room of the family. Everything went on there—cooking, baby-tending, washing, social life. Then, as families became richer and more genteel and began to have servants to do the work, the kitchen was relegated to the back of the house where it wouldn't be seen. Meals were eaten in the dining room, and entertaining was done in the parlor.

Time passed, and servants became scarce and expensive, and the American housewife had to do her own work again. Still the standards of the previous era remained, and the kitchen was used only for cooking and washing.

Then, as women began to have outside jobs, the kitchen became a streamlined kitchenette, designed to save labor, so small that you could reach everything in it without moving a step.

Now times are changing again. The kitchen is getting bigger. Family and guests like to be with the housewife while she is working, and what's more, she wants them there to help out. Families eat in the kitchen, teen-agers give parties there, fathers help with the dishes, children play there. The home-maker wants a desk for planning, maybe a laundry, a rest corner and a sewing center. The kitchen is becoming an activity room again.

The rest of the house is changing to match. In many homes the parlor has given way to a room that is living room, work room and play room combined. Maybe the kitchen is part of it too, separated from the dining area by low cabinets or storage walls. The bedroom is no longer expected to hold only a bed, a chair and a dresser. It may be used for study, sitting room and workshop. The cellar is not just a coal hole and a furnace. It can be laundry, canning and freezing center, workshop and meeting room for the Boy Scout troop.

This means that a house may have to be changed around inside so that its original builder wouldn't recognize it.

You can do it if you will remember some basic rules.

1. The first and most important rule is: *be guided by convenience, not convention.*

A room that was built for a dining room doesn't have to be used for a dining room. It can be a study, an extra living room, a bedroom, anything you like. On the other hand, just because the latest books tell you that the dining room is on the way out, don't feel you can't have one if you like it. There is something very comfortable about a big table with chairs around it—a table that is always there and doesn't have to be unfolded, and chairs that don't have to be fetched from all the corners of the room. There is a feeling of peace and quiet about a room that is used just for dining, with no cooking odors or view of dirty dishes.

But if you have to use a room for an unusual purpose, don't try to do it with conventional furniture or storage arrangements. If you must use a living room to sleep in, of course you won't keep a regular bed in it. You'll get a studio bed. You'll try to plan chests and cupboards designed to go with the living room furniture and big enough to hold clothes, blankets and whatever else you need for sleeping and dressing, so that the room can be turned into a bedroom or back into a living room with the fewest possible motions and trips.

2. The second rule is: *consider the personalities and habits of your family, yourself included.* These can be changed and influenced if necessary. Don't do it if it isn't necessary, because then you lose strength when it is.

It's no use fixing up a lovely playroom in the attic if the children are going to keep dragging their toys down and leaving them in the living room and kitchen and hall, everywhere but in the attic, where you say they belong. Better have a conference with them and come to some agreement so they won't think that keeping toys out of the kitchen is just some grown-up whim of yours.

It's no use arranging a lovely sewing corner in the bedroom

for yourself if you are never going to sew there, but *will* keep taking your things into the living room to be with the family. Admit to yourself that this is what you prefer to do, and arrange for it.

3. *Consider the possibilities of the situation.* The book may say it is good to have a corner of the kitchen for the baby to play in, or that Dad likes to be with you when he comes home from the office. If the kitchen is very small it may be impossible.

4. *Consider the working conditions offered by any location for a particular job.* Maybe a certain spot in the living room is ideal for a desk. It is an alcove and the desk looks just darling there. But there is no daylight, so you can't use it in the daytime, and in the evening the family makes a lot of noise and won't keep quiet no matter how you scold. Obviously this is not the place for the desk.

Now draw a floor plan to scale of your house or apartment. Make little two-dimensional scale models of your furniture out of cardboard so you can move them about on the floor plan. Make your plan big enough to include shelves, closets and other storage places and indicate what goes in them. Show all the windows and doors, and draw the arcs that show which way the doors swing. Indicate directions so you will know which windows get the morning sun, which are the southern exposures that are good for living rooms and nurseries in winter, which get a north light that is good for summer and for painting, and which are warmed by the afternoon sun and give a view of the sunset.

Now you are ready to put in your activities and the equipment that goes with them.

Certain activities are basic to every family. No matter how our customs differ, we all need some sort of living room for resting, conversation, reading, writing, playing, entertainment. We all need sleeping quarters, a place for bathing, dressing and other personal care, and space to store our possessions. We all prepare food, which means storing, cooking, serving, eating and cleaning up. We all need work space for laundry, for repairs, for hobbies, for study, for odd jobs of all kinds. And we need traffic lanes to reach all these areas and extra space for storage.

Decide which of these things you and your family do, and think of all the other things you do that haven't been mentioned. Do you listen to records, keep a dog, raise fish, come home from skating and drink cocoa, read in front of the fire, typewrite, make furniture, hold meetings, enlarge pictures, collect stamps, write novels, run a real estate office in your home? You have to find room in the house for all these activities, and you must try to manage so that they don't interfere with each other.

You can make a chart on a large piece of brown paper. On one side, under the four main categories, QUIET ACTIVITIES, LIVING, FEEDING, and WORKING, list all your family occupations. On the other side list all the rooms in your house. Then draw lines from the activities to the room where they take place. Along the connecting lines, write the names of the family members involved in the activities.

On the facing page you can see how the chart will look, filled out for an imaginary family named Reed.

Now on your floor plan you can put into each room the furniture that goes with the activities listed for that room.

Some of your activities will fall naturally into certain fixed places. Cooking and dishwashing are done in the kitchen. Bathing is done in the bathroom, sleeping in the bedrooms, entertaining in the living room.

But in any home, no matter how small, you have some choice. You may have an outdoor grill for summer cooking. Then you will store some utensils near an exit or in the basement where they can be quickly taken out on a tray or a wheeled cart. If you have a terrace opening off the kitchen or living room, this will influence the placing of furniture because you'll want to keep traffic lanes free for carrying food and drinks outdoors.

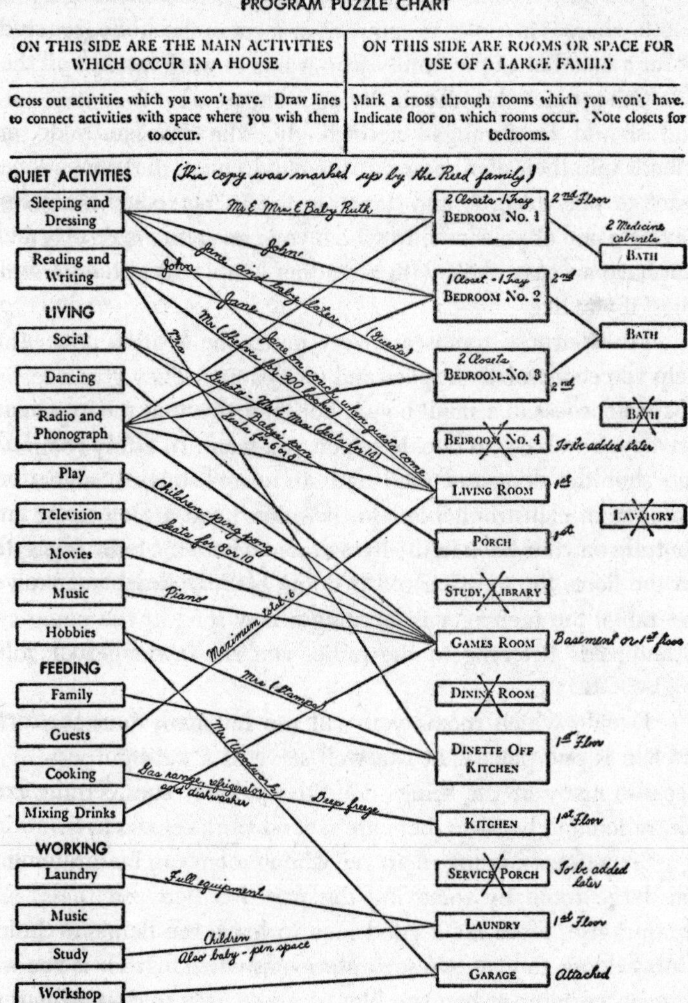
PROGRAM PUZZLE CHART
ON THIS SIDE ARE THE MAIN ACTIVITIES WHICH OCCUR IN A HOUSE
ON THIS SIDE ARE ROOMS OR SPACE FOR USE OF A LARGE FAMILY
Cross out activities which you won't have. Draw lines to connect activities with space where you wish them to occur.
Mark a cross through rooms which you won't have. Indicate floor on which rooms occur. Note closets for bedrooms.
QUIET ACTIVITIES
(This copy was marked up by the Reed family)
Sleeping and Dressing
Reading and Writing
LIVING
Social
Dancing
Radio and Phonograph
Play
Television
Movies
Music
Hobbies
FEEDING
Family
Guests
Cooking
Mixing Drinks
WORKING
Laundry
Music
Study
Workshop
Office
2 Closets-1 Tray
BEDROOM No. 1
2nd Floor
2 Medicine cabinets
BATH
1 Closet-1 Tray
BEDROOM No. 2
2nd
BATH
2 Closets
BEDROOM No. 3
2nd
BATH
BEDROOM No. 4
To be added later
LIVING ROOM
1st
LAVATORY
PORCH
1st
STUDY, LIBRARY
GAMES ROOM
Basement or 1st floor
DINING ROOM
DINETTE OFF KITCHEN
1st Floor
KITCHEN
1st Floor
SERVICE PORCH
To be added later
LAUNDRY
1st Floor
GARAGE
Attached
Mr & Mrs & Baby Ruth
John
Jane and baby later
Jane
(Guests)
Jane on couch when guests come
Children-ping pong
Seats for 8 or 10
Piano
Maximum total 6
Mrs (Stamps)
Gas range, refrigerator and dishwasher
Deep freeze
Full equipment
Children
Also baby-pen space

Reprinted with permission from Catherine and Harold R. Sleeper, *The House for You to Build, Buy or Rent,* John Wiley & Sons, Inc. New York, 1949, p. 156.

You may have sleeping places for occasional use, such as a porch where it is cooler in summer, or a cot in the study for a guest or for a member of the family who wants to work late.

Other places besides the living room are used for entertaining and should be arranged accordingly. The children take their friends into their own rooms. If the children are in their teens and want to play records and dance in the living room, you should have a place of your own to which you can retire, and where you can have an easy chair with a reading lamp, and also entertain a guest if you like.

Multipurpose rooms are very much the fashion now. They help you economize on space and on cleaning. They give a feeling of spaciousness in a small house, but they give it at the expense of privacy. You have to decide which you want. In a tiny room you can shut the door and read and study undisturbed, unless you suffer from claustrophobia. On the other hand, if you try to concentrate on your book in the living room where the baby is playing on the floor, the ten-year-old is doing his homework out loud at the table, the teen-ager is learning a new song at the piano and Grandma is listening to the radio, you are in danger of going mad.

Decide which rooms you will use for many purposes. The kitchen is one place that can well serve as a multipurpose room because many of the things done there don't require quiet concentration and because there are several work centers in it.

Sometimes a living room and dining room can be thrown into one large room by removing the partition between them, and contrariwise, often it's a good idea to leave the doors, or install sliding doors, to give two separate rooms when privacy is needed. Screens, curtains or bamboo blinds can be used to shut off part of a room. Screens are useful too in shutting out light or hiding work areas like kitchens, or unsightly things like pipes, but of course they don't keep out noise.

When two children share a bedroom they will often be happier if they can have some sort of movable partition between them, which can be pushed back when they want a big play space and closed when they want to be alone. It sometimes helps, if they can't have rooms of their own, to make a wall of furniture by putting bookcases and chests of drawers down the middle of the room. You can decorate the backs of the pieces with each child's favorite pictures. Then the occupant of each side will at least *feel* that he's in his own castle even if he can still hear the one on the other side.

Your home must contain not only work places, but rest and play places, and if you use multipurpose rooms be sure they are arranged to make all three possible. When you push aside the sliding doors or the bamboo blinds which have made a work corner for you, can you really dance or play games, or must you first roll up the rug, move heavy furniture and take a lot of glass animals and porcelain statuettes out of the way?

Try to furnish such a room with small rugs, lightweight furniture, and as little bric-a-brac as possible. Plan where you will put the chairs and tables you shove out of the way, so the room doesn't look too messy when it is being used for play. You can't have a good time in a room that looks like moving day. And try to store the games and card tables in files or racks so you needn't disarrange them all to get at a particular one.

If you live in a house that has a garden or terrace or porch which you use as an outdoor living room, see that it is arranged so that you can enjoy it with a minimum of effort. If you have to go out the front door lugging folding chairs, tables, umbrellas, and cushions, traipse all the way around to the back, set up your gear in a shady spot, and then half an hour later have to move because you are now in the sun or because you aren't shielded from a chilly breeze, you will probably tend to stay in the house where it's more comfortable. A screened porch, furniture that can be left outdoors, a roof or awning that will always provide shade, and a terrace placed in the lee of the house where you can count on being sheltered from the prevailing wind are worth thinking about when you plan your layout.

Consider travel and traffic very carefully. Make note of the number of times you go from one place to another. Make a list of these trips in your notebook. Here are some typical trips:

Bedroom to bath
Bedroom to kitchen
Bedroom to nursery
Kitchen to children's room
Kitchen to front door
Any part of the house to front door
Kitchen to dining room
Dining room to kitchen
Kitchen to laundry
Laundry to drying yard
Kitchen to heating plant
Heating plant to outdoors with ashes (if it's a coal furnace)
Front door to living room
Indoors to outdoor living room
Garage to house
Any part of house to telephone

In making any of these routine trips, do you have to walk around obstacles like furniture or partitions or other people? Do you have to make so many steps and detours that you heave a sigh when the doorbell or the telephone rings?

The location of the telephone is often a problem. The bedroom is a convenient place because it is private. But if there are more than two in the family you don't want them all traipsing in and out of your bedroom. And you may not want to be startled out of your sleep by the phone ringing in your ear. The living room is a good central place but it is hard to hold a conversation with many people in the room. The hall is good, but there may be no room to sit down. If you wish to limit conversation this may be a point in favor of the hall, but usually you like to sit when you talk on the phone. A phone in the kitchen is handy but think of the nuisance of having the family cluttering up the place by the hour, especially if you have teen-agers!

Perhaps you'll decide on a telephone in the living room with a long cord so it can be taken into the hall. Or you may have an extension in the kitchen which can be shut off when you don't want to be bothered. Or have a hole cut in the wall between kitchen and living room, so the phone can be reached from either place.

Think of the sequence of jobs and plan for ease in going from one to the next. The commonest example is the location of the bathroom right next to the bedroom. You tumble out of bed and into the shower, or out of the bathtub and into bed, as the case may be.

If you eat in the living room, have the table at the wall nearest the kitchen.

If you must constantly leave the kitchen to go to the nursery, have a play or sleeping place for the baby in a corner of the kitchen or in a room close by, or outdoors just outside the window or door. If a child is sick, see if you can't move him to a room next the kitchen.

Note on your floor plan, in dotted lines of different colors, the main traffic routes in your home, and observe where they go. Be sure you don't have traffic lanes going through your work centers or conversation groups. Arrange your furniture if necessary so that people walk behind a sofa rather than between it and an easy chair. Don't put a piece of furniture—a chair, a table, a bookcase—in a natural traffic lane, unless the object is so shallow that it won't be bumped into. Notice if you bump anything. Sometimes you don't realize till you see a black and blue spot on yourself that you have been hitting against a protruding corner.

Don't have traffic lanes going in front of television sets. Modern homes must provide space for radio and television entertainment as well as for home movies. This means being able to shift seats without too much confusion.

See that there is plenty of space on all sides of furniture for cleaning, for opening and closing windows, for getting books from bookcases, for bed making.

See that your entrances and exits are clear and convenient. Is there a shelter over each entrance, as well as a door mat on the floor? Is the entrance screened from the living room so the family need not be disturbed by salesmen or messengers? Is there a coat closet near the entrance, as well as a mirror for putting on hats, and a bench to sit on while donning rubbers?

It is very convenient, if you have the space, to have some sort of receiving center for parcels, groceries, clothes from the cleaner, laundry, mail. A counter with shelves above and hangers at the side is very nice, but a small table will serve if that's all you have room for. Be sure there's a pad and pencil on it. A partitioned box for incoming and outgoing mail is useful at the front door.

In a well-planned house you shouldn't have to carry coal or ashes or garden equipment through the kitchen. There should be a separate basement entrance. And it's nice to be able to get from the garage to the house without getting wet.

Some of your rooms may have too many doors. This is often true in old houses where one room opens into another, making a room into a passageway. Try to shut off some of these doors. You will get more wall space and reduce irritation. But if it is impossible to shut a door, you may be able to eliminate the traffic lane by setting up furniture as a suggested partition.

The newest floor plans are designed to give what are called "dead end rooms." That is, no room opens into another, but all open on to a central hall. Not only is wall space saved, but also floor space, for no part of any room has to be used as a passageway.

No hall should be any longer than is absolutely necessary, unless it is meant to be used as a room. Many old houses have yards of hallway that is useless and cuts off light and circulation of air. Sometimes the ends of these halls can be partitioned off to make closets. If the house is your own and you are free to tear down walls, you can cut out some of these halls and throw the space thus freed into extra room space.

Kitchen layout is so important, and so much research has been done about it, that it deserves a division to itself.

Just to show how much good arrangement means, a woman in Iowa performed an experiment. She strapped a pedometer to her ankle and wore it for a week while doing her kitchen work. She found she was walking an average of five miles a day or 1825 miles a year. By rearranging her major pieces of equipment she reduced her hiking to two and a half miles a day, and in addition saved an hour's time each day.

Of course you may not be in a position to rearrange your sink, stove or refrigerator. Moving any of these is a major operation. If you're living in a rented house it may be impossible, and even if the house is your own it may be too expensive, though when you consider how many steps you can save, you may want to fix up the kitchen and save on something else.

If you're building or renovating, you are in luck. Now is your chance to have a really efficient kitchen.

First, you must be very sure to figure out the best arrangements. Take your floor plan and place your little scale models on it, either the way the kitchen is set up now or the way you think you'd like to have it. Now make believe you are getting a meal in the kitchen. Be very realistic about it. Actually plan your menu and decide how you would go about cooking the dinner. Suppose you have meat loaf, mashed potatoes, string beans, green salad, chocolate pudding, bread and butter and milk.

Write down the number of times you go to the sink, to the stove, to the refrigerator, to the mix center, to the dining area with dishes for the table. You will find, as other researchers have found, that the sink center is the most used. You make more trips to it than to any other center. You use it for vegetable preparation, for dishwashing, to get water for cooking, to drain cooked foods. You will need a counter on either side of the sink bowl.

The second most important center is the stove. You need a counter beside it too.

Third in point of use comes the mix center. This is a table or counter at which you prepare desserts, salad, meat loaf, baked goods.

The refrigerator is fourth in importance, and the eating center ranks about the same. You must decide where this experimental meal will be eaten—in the kitchen or in the dining room. Of course, your final arrangement will take both into consideration.

There should be a counter next to the handle of the refrigerator, so that you can put down the dishes you take from it, and there should be another counter near the china cabinet so you can set a tray down and fill it.

Now where should you put these different centers? You'll find you make the most trips between the sink and the range centers, so they ought to be close together, with a counter between. They can be side by side, or at right angles to each other.

The second largest number of trips is made between the mix center and the sink. So it would seem that you ought to place the sink first, and then locate the mix center and the range conveniently near, perhaps one on either side. As the sink is the hardest to move once it is in place, think very carefully about it. If you are remodeling, you will find it simplest to leave the sink where it is and shift the other pieces.

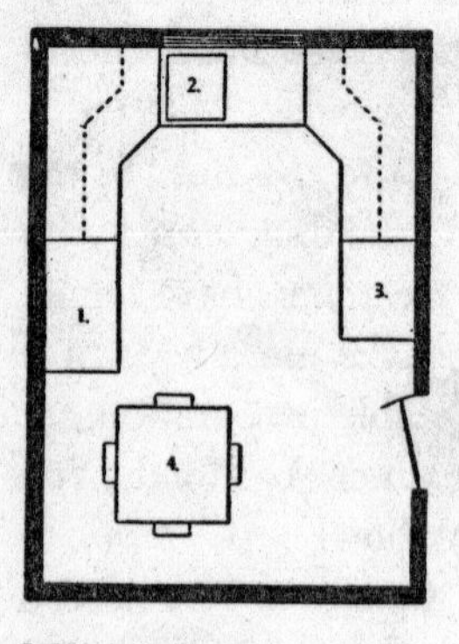

Your kitchen may be arranged in the form of a U, in which case the sink might be at the bottom of the U, the mix center at right angles to it on the right, and the range at right angles on the left.

1. Range. 2. Sink. 3. Refrigerator. 4. Table. Dotted lines show front of upper cabinets.

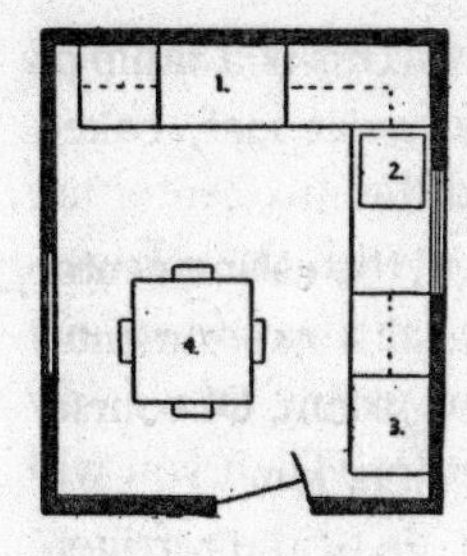

It may be L-shaped, with the sink and mix center on one wall and the stove on the other.

1. Range. 2. Sink. 3. Refrigerator. 4. Table. Dotted lines show front of upper cabinets.

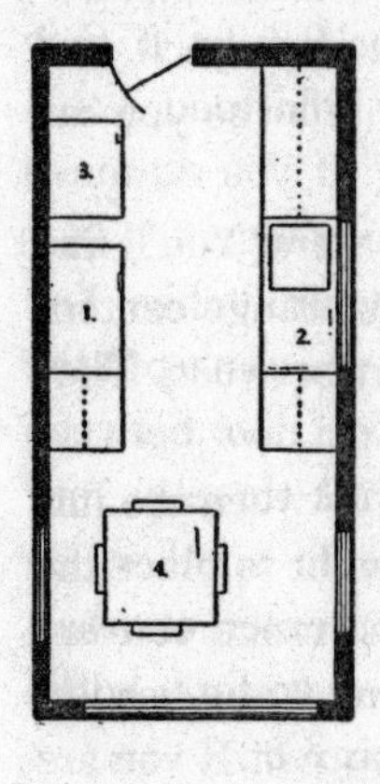

You may have a two-walled or corridor kitchen, with the sink against one wall and the range opposite. Or you may have a strip kitchen with all three centers along one wall. This is the least convenient but it takes up the least space, and is often used in very small kitchens.

A U-shaped kitchen is very economical of steps, since there are two right angles in it, which shortens the distance between your centers. Unless you are the only person using it, however, or unless it is very large, you will find yourself bumping into other people who are working with you. Of course if the kitchen is very large, the U-shaped kitchen will be wasteful of steps. In this case it is better to have one of your centers extending into the middle of the room as an island rather than to have them all spread around the edges. You can have the range center as the island, forming a low partition between the kitchen and the dining center. This makes a convenient serving arrangement.

The L-shaped kitchen uses two walls for equipment and

leaves the other two free for dining table, passageway, play pen, rest center, or whatever else you want to put in.

You will find that the sink, the range, and the mix center are all used to about the same extent in connection with the refrigerator. So try to place your refrigerator not too far away from any of them. It is a good thing if you can put your eating area fairly close to both the china center and the refrigerator. Then you will find it easy to set the table.

A good deal depends on the habits of your family. If they drink much milk or ice water or eat much very cold food, you'll use the ice box more in connection with serving. If you do much baking you may want the mix center very near the range.

Much depends too on the size and shape of your kitchen. You may have so many doors and windows in it that you can't put the pieces where you would like them. Try not to have a door between two pieces of equipment. If you do, you will walk three or four feet unnecessarily every time you go from one to another. Be sure your refrigerator door opens *toward* the mix center, or whatever counter it is near. If it doesn't, every time you go for a bottle of milk or the butter dish you will walk an extra six feet.

Many doors in a kitchen means that people will use the room as a passageway. Don't allow this. Nothing is worse than to have somebody barge through just as you are taking the roast out of the oven or draining the spaghetti into the sink. Shut off some of the doors. If you must have traffic lanes, be sure they are at the edge of the kitchen.

Too many windows cut down wall space and make it hard to place equipment in the best positions. A stove, for instance, can't be placed in front of a window that is to be opened. Curtains cannot be hung near a stove. You can't put cupboards or shelves where there is a window. A refrigerator is too tall to go under a window.

You may have to close one or two windows permanently. Of course, a kitchen must have light, and the closed windows will still admit light, but be careful about the shades you use. They must be noninflammable and easily operated.

Since you spend so much time at the sink, it's nice to have a window over it, so you can rest your eyes by looking out (preferably at a beautiful view).

Be sure you plan space in the kitchen for your wheeled table. This can sometimes be garaged under a table or an overhanging shelf, to keep odds and ends from being piled on it. See that you have enough aisle space to wheel it, and that the floor is smooth and free from sills and steps. This isn't always possible in an old house, but a floor that is continuous and uninterrupted is a boon to the housekeeper, and worth taking some trouble to get.

Studies were made at the Motion and Time Study Laboratory at Purdue University, in which the three types of kitchens were compared. A meal for four people was prepared in each kitchen. The researchers found that the U-shaped kitchen required the smallest number of feet of travel (about 450), the L-shaped kitchen was next with about 490, and the strip kitchen required about 760. The job also took the least time in the U-shaped kitchen.*

However, as we said before, the U-type is sometimes awkward for more than one person to work in. Some students feel that the L-shaped room is better because it allows for traffic which does not interfere with the work centers.

The broken U is a compromise between these two types. This was the form chosen by the New York Heart Association for its demonstration kitchen. The plan of this kitchen is given in Chapter 4.

You can see that in designing this kitchen account was taken of the sequence of jobs. Meal preparation being the most important job, food supplies are brought in and stored on the shelves (10) and in the refrigerator (8), whence they go to the mix center

* *Easier Homemaking,* Station Bulletin 529, Agricultural Experiment Station, Purdue University, Lafayette, Indiana, 1948.

(7), the sink center (3), and the stove (12). Since food is served from the stove and dishes are returned to the sink, these two centers are conveniently placed near the entrance to the dinette.

Cabinets for storage are arranged above and below the different work centers, to make full use of the principle of storage at the point of first use. Dishes and tools used most frequently were stored within elbow reach. Groceries were stored in single file on narrow shelves. The stove had a high oven to eliminate stooping and there was a wheeled table stored under a shelf beside the stove. The dinette is large enough to be used both as an eating center and as a planning and relaxation center.

Below is another plan showing the direction in which activities move. It was designed as a farm kitchen and workroom, and it is much larger than anything most of us would need or be able to have, but it is useful for showing how traffic can be routed. The room at the right is a utility and laundry room, and it contains a food preservation center and freezer. In the kitchen proper, the refrigerator is at the right, near the door, handy for storing food brought in from outside. There is a pass through to the freezer. Next comes the mix counter and then the sink. The stove is at right angles to the sink and between them is a work counter with a pass through to the dinette. When clearing-up time comes, the dishes are sent back to the sink through this opening or over the top of the stove. The garbage disposal can is at the right of the sink, and there is a door opening to the outdoors so that the garbage can need not be carried through the kitchen. Food to be put away after the meal is set on the mix counter nearest the refrigerator.

Miscellaneous storage is along the wall opposite the sink so that the traffic will not interfere with the main job of meal-getting. In one corner of the dinette is a center for sewing and relaxation, while in the opposite corner there is room for children to play where they can be under their mother's supervision yet not underfoot.*

* U.S. Dept. of Agriculture, Home and Garden Bulletin, No. 12.

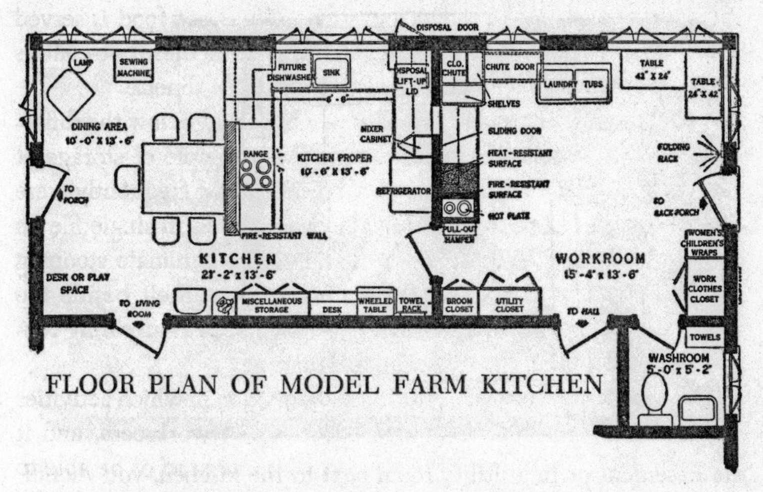

FLOOR PLAN OF MODEL FARM KITCHEN

Laundry layout is important too, especially in a home where there are small children and washing is done three or four times a week or more. Most of us who live in apartments or ready-built small homes do our washing in the kitchen, where the layout consists of a sink or washing machine, near which we store our laundry supplies, and perhaps a drying rack or a line out of the window. If you are arranging a separate laundry, however, whether it is in

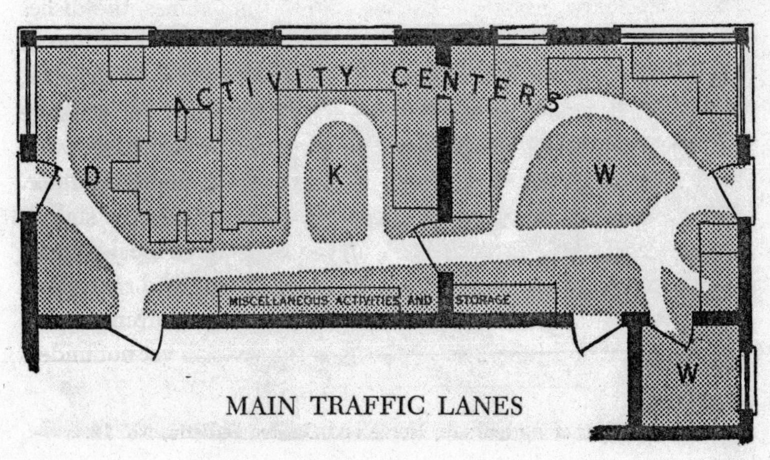

MAIN TRAFFIC LANES

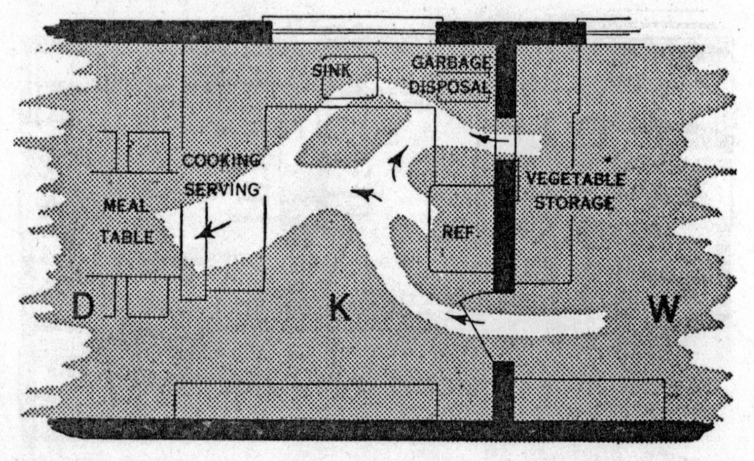

the basement or in a utility room next to the kitchen, you should try to arrange your equipment according to the sequence of jobs.

First, clothes are brought to the laundry and must be sorted, spots removed, mending done. This means you need a hamper or bags for the soiled clothes, and a table for sorting. If the table is on wheels it can be used later in another location for sprinkling.

Then the clothes are washed, which includes bleaching, bluing, rinsing and perhaps starching. You need stationary tubs and

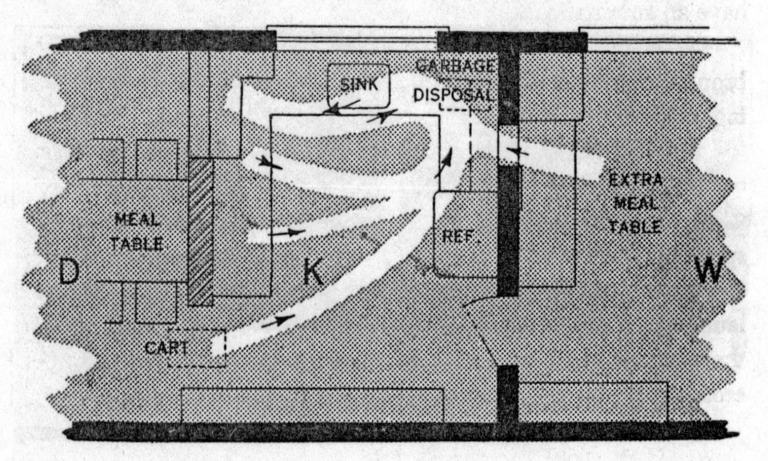

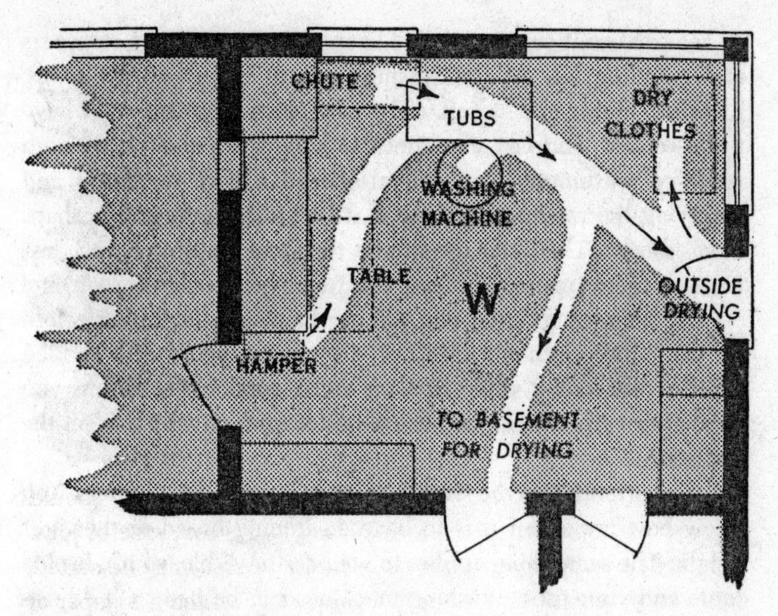

perhaps a washing machine and a stove for making starch and for boiling clothes.

Then you need a cart or basket to take the clothes to the drying area, either outdoors or indoors, unless you are lucky enough to have an automatic dryer.

After the clothes are dry, the direction is reversed. They are brought back in the cart or basket, sorted for folding or dampening on a table or counter, and then ironed.

The ironing equipment consists of a board, an iron or electric ironer, a rack for finished clothes and a chair to sit on.

This means you will have four centers: a sorting, mending, spot-removing center (which we will call a "treatment" center); a washing center, a drying center, and an ironing center. The laundry plan in the farm kitchen shown above is so arranged that the work can follow a well-planned route, with no backtracking or crossing of work paths.

At each center you should store the things you will use there.

At the treatment center you will keep the spot and stain removers and mending kit. At the washing center there will be soaps, bleaches, bluing and starch. (The new plastic starches don't have to be cooked, and last sometimes as long as six months, through repeated washings.) You will also need a hose for filling and emptying the washing machine if it isn't automatic, and perhaps a washboard. The latter used to be the chief feature of washday, but now there are actually some children who have never seen one!

At the ironing center you will need a plastic bag or tablecloth for dampened clothes, a sprinkler, a sponge or bottle with padded top for dampening while ironing, and a press cloth. Unless you have an iron that tilts, you need asbestos mats on which to set the hot iron.

Pay attention to the work heights in your various centers. You know how important it is to have an ironing board of the right height. The same thing applies to your sorting table, your wheeled table and your tubs. Washing machines can be had with adjustable legs, or you can get a top-loading machine to prevent stooping. Clothes lines may be hung low enough to save reaching, or indoor racks can be used that fold up when they're not needed.

How you dry your clothes depends on the climate and the surroundings. If you live in a warm, dry, clean place you may always hang your clothes outdoors. But most of us need some sort of indoor drying place if there is much rain or soot.

It's wonderful to have a dryer and an ironer. Whether you do or not depends on how much you can spend, how much you will use them, and whether your house is equipped for them.

In 1951, of 44 million homes, 30 million had washing machines, three and three-quarter million had ironers, and fewer than one million had dryers.

To accommodate the most modern laundry equipment you need not only the space, but the right kind of floor, water supply, drainage and electric circuits. A firm and solid floor is needed for this heavy equipment. A modern automatic washer uses a great deal of hot water and you may need to install a heater. And it is usually necessary to put in some extra wiring to take care of the electricity requirements of a heater, a dryer and an ironer.

The workroom is a wonderful place for other jobs besides laundry. Since you don't wash every day, the other jobs can be fitted in nicely and need not interfere with the daily work of getting meals, as they might do in the kitchen. Food can be canned or prepared for freezing here. Furniture can be painted and upholstered, radios tinkered with, toys mended. It's a good place for the cleaning closet and for hanging outdoor wraps.

If you have space for the combination kitchen and workroom you may find your family living in it and neglecting the rest of the house entirely, because it's so easy to be sociable here, especially if there's an old sofa to relax on and some bright paint and curtains to take away the white-tiled kitchen look.

You can get a great deal of help and many valuable ideas for good kitchen and laundry layout by writing to the United States Department of Agriculture, which has done a wonderful job of preparing bulletins on the subject. Nearly all the state universities, too, have agricultural extension services which are doing research on home planning and management, and will send you literature and working drawings, or tell you where to get them.

Chapter 8

Making Changes—Working Conditions

Layout is more than arranging rooms in a house or furniture in a room. It means also having the right conditions for each activity that goes on in the house.

Working conditions in industry are very carefully studied. In the right setup, workers are happier, feel better and produce more. In our homes we aren't always so thoughtful.

Some situations demand quiet. Sleep, for instance. You can get used to sleeping through noise, but it isn't really restful. A peaceful atmosphere is needed for reading, writing and studying.

If you can't bring quiet to the places you have chosen for these activities, you may have to put them somewhere else. Try to locate your quiet workroom and your sleeping place away from noise sources. Bathrooms and kitchens are such, and so are children, telephones, radios, outdoor traffic, elevators, music rooms, workshops. Try to have the quiet activities on the other side of the house or separated from the noise source by closets or a stairwell to keep the noise out.

Sometimes you want to keep noise *in* a room to protect other rooms. Or you may want to minimize the noise for those in the room. Acoustical ceilings and walls are a great help in music rooms or workshops where machinery is used. Hangings, rugs, insulation, even beaverboard absorb and deaden sound.

Noise is annoying to practically everybody who is trying to do any work that requires concentration. Some experiments show that a noisy background sometimes seems to be stimulating, but still it exerts wear and tear on nerves and so ought to be eliminated as far as possible.

Some noises are more bothersome than others. Continuous, monotonous noises like the tick of a clock or the rumble of traffic gradually become part of the background and don't seem to be noticed, but the cumulative effect is tiring, as we realize with relief when they stop. Interrupted, intermittent noises, like the occasional rattle of a shade or the squeak of a door or toot of a horn can be very disturbing. Of course a noise heard against the background of quiet is more disturbing than when it is somewhat deadened by other sounds.

Often people dislike a particular work area because of the noise in it. A creaking hinge or a dripping faucet or a machine that needs oiling may be all that bothers you.

Sometimes you realize that the noise is inescapable and get resigned to it. This is a great help as it saves you the trouble of doing anything about it. Such a conclusion is all right if it's your children's play or your husband's typing that you get used to. But don't carry this attitude too far or you will find yourself putting up with all kinds of annoyances which it is the province of this book to help you remove.

We all say we long for quiet. But some work areas are not good because they are *too quiet.* Jobs that don't require concentration may come to be disliked because they are lonely. This is a frequent cause of dissatisfaction in housework. Maybe you can do something about it.

A hobby room or general workroom where several people can work together makes for great sociability. People don't have to be helping each other or working at the same task; it is enough that they are in the same room. Perhaps you can set up a blackboard or play table in the kitchen for your youngster. We usually take it for granted that it is good for our children to be with us. We forget how good it is for us to be with them until they grow up and go away about their own affairs.

Sometimes scheduling combined with a change of layout will help. You can plan to iron or sew or knit in the living room when the family are at home, and do the work that must be done in some other part of the house when you are alone.

If you feel lonely in the kitchen, move the radio in there. Some people even get a dog or a canary bird just to have some noise around the house. Some borrow the neighbors' children, or go in for co-operative housekeeping, or have groups of young people in for club meetings or parties. Any such projects, of course, involve many changes in your housekeeping arrangements.

Physical surroundings affect us all. You may hate to work in the basement because you dislike the drab color of the walls, the pipes overhead, and the small windows and naked bulbs hanging from the ceiling. This is a matter of decoration. Some cheerful paint and a good light fixture will make a lot of difference. Maybe you hate it because it is messy. Simply organizing the area as a work space will make it look better, since the truly functional is always satisfying to the eye.

Make a floor plan of the basement and lay out the different work and play areas in it. You may have a laundry, game room, dance floor, workshop, photo studio, storage place for canned goods, furnace room. Throw out the assorted cardboard boxes, bushel baskets and old tin cans that have accumulated. Make containers for the bits of wood and nails and wire that the carpenter of the family may find useful.

Partitioning off the entertainment center may shut out the more unsightly laundry and workshop, but it may also cut off ventilation, light, and the view of the prettier portion for the person who works there. Movable screens may be the answer to this, to be pushed aside when the wash is being done.

Color is important in any workroom—the colors that you like and that make you feel at ease. Don't feel constrained by what you read about certain tones being restful and others stimulating. One person may feel that gray and blue are soothing colors; another may find them depressing. Some like red and yellow and find them stimulating; others wish you would take them away.

Arrange your workroom with regard to what is outside the window as well as inside. Everybody knows how refreshing it is to work in a room with a view, and how depressing to look out on a brick wall across a narrow courtyard.

The floors of your home deserve some thought. They should be smooth, easily cleaned, not slippery, resilient, and durable. Actually, the perfect flooring has not yet been invented, but there are a great many on the market that fill the bill pretty well as you can see by consulting some of the books and pamphlets that are published on house construction and decorating.

Wood, of course, is the most conventional flooring. In living rooms, bedrooms, and so on, hard wood is used, and this has to be shellacked and waxed at intervals. If well treated it lasts indefinitely.

In kitchens linoleum has long been the favorite. There are many different kinds, from the inexpensive enameled felt-back material to the inlaid kind which is expensive but with good care will last fifteen to twenty years. They are easy underfoot and easily washed, but they must be very carefully laid so no water can get underneath, or they may buckle and rot; besides, they have to be kept waxed and they may be slippery when wet or overwaxed.

Concrete wears well and so do tile and brick but they are very hard on the feet—cold and without resilience.

Cork tile is quiet, comfortable and safe, easy to clean, a good insulator, and attractive, but it isn't grease resistant so it isn't usually used in kitchens and besides it's extremely expensive.

There is a new plastic resilient flooring that seems to be smooth, nonporous and durable, and resistant to water, oil, acid, alcohol, fire and many other things. It's easy to care for (doesn't need waxing) and comes in a wide range of colors. The initial cost is said to be high, but if everything else that is said about it is true, it would be worth saving up for.

Some people are sensitive to odors in or around their workrooms. If you are one of those people, find out what the odors come from. Sometimes a soap or disinfectant or paint has a very annoying smell and another kind may be substituted. Odors are especially sharp during pregnancy and you can make yourself happier if you get rid of the unpleasant ones and surround yourself with the ones you like. If the odor comes from garbage or a compost pile or a dumbwaiter that isn't kept clean, or from plumbing, or a damp cellar, do something about it. These smells are not only unpleasant, they point to an unsanitary condition.

Some people don't like the smell of the things they work with, such as rubber goods, leather, paper, ink, furniture polish and certain plastics. In these days of deodorants, when even your dog is supposed to get rid of a doggy odor by eating food with chlorophyll in it, nobody need be offended by smells, unless they work in a chemical factory or happen to be mothproofing. And as long as you're sure the smell doesn't come from anything unhealthy, remove it with one of those little bottles that sit on a shelf and erase odors.

Sometimes work areas are unpleasant to the sense of touch. Gritty or rough walls; wet, slippery floors or counters; corners that collect dust or grease; handles on tools that have become rough or sticky; cold things to be handled (as in the deep freeze); wet things outdoors in winter (pails or garbage cans); messy things (fowl to be cleaned); hot things (the old-fashioned coal range, or any oven that lets a blast of hot air out in your face); all these can be very annoying.

Some of them are unavoidable. If so, make the best of it. If not, remedy them. In any case know what it is that you don't like, and try to keep the unpleasant feeling from spreading to other activities.

A workroom must have *proper ventilation, heat, humidity and freedom from dust.* You can't work well without plenty of clean fresh air, which should be neither too hot nor too cold. Extreme heat and cold are both debilitating, and the temperature should remain even.

Kitchens and laundries get too hot and steamy. Other parts of our houses get too hot and dry in winter, and we wonder why we feel sluggish.

For some people, an air conditioner in summer is as important as a furnace in winter. But air conditioners are still very expensive. A unit for a single room costs upward of $300 to install and $15 a month to operate. For a six room house the installation may cost around $1800, and about $50 a month to run. The latter of course can heat the house as well as cool it, so it's good for year-round use. It is a fine investment if you can afford it, because it filters dust from the air and keeps the atmosphere moist. It cuts out a lot of cleaning and dusting, and might pay for itself in time in savings on maid service and cleaning bills.

There are other systems of cleansing and moving the air—filters, screens and fans—which are less expensive and which may be all you need. If you install an electric fan in your kitchen window and put cloth screens in your other windows, the fan will suck filtered air in from outside and blow odors and stale air out.

Radiant heating keeps your house a lot cleaner than furnaces and hot air systems.

A fireplace is nice for sociability, and for an occasional chilly day, but can't be depended on for heating.

Investigate all types of heating, cooling, ventilating and humidifying systems and do all you can to be comfortable.

Good lighting is one of the most important working conditions, and one most frequently neglected and misunderstood. Daylight is the best light there is, and should always be used whenever possible.

Of course every one of us has heard from early childhood the words: "Don't read in a bad light," often accompanied by threats of having to wear glasses or worse. Many of us go right on working or reading or just sitting in a bad light, partly because we don't know what bad light does to us, and partly because we don't understand what constitutes a good light.

A great deal of study has been done to find out what good seeing conditions are, and many interesting facts have been brought to light (no pun).

The greatest number of eye defects—from plain eyestrain to actual disease—is found among people who do close eye work indoors. Among farmers and laborers, for instance, only from one to twenty per cent have eye defects. Among carpenters, painters, machinists and printers the number goes up. From 60% to 80% of housewives and scholars have some sort of eye trouble, and among draftsmen and stenographers the astonishing total is from 80% to 100%.

More and more school children and college students are obliged to wear glasses. The tendency to hold the book close to the eyes to overcome insufficient light is a primary cause of nearsightedness.

Strangely enough, the eyes don't give us warning right away. If you're lifting a load which is too heavy, your arm and your back tell you at once. But the eye adjusts itself so quickly and automatically that we never notice the strain of trying to see in semi-darkness or extreme brightness, or the thousands of tiny motions involved in looking from a bright object to a dark one, from a sunny window to a deep shadow.

For good seeing, you must have the right quantity of light as well as the right quality.

Engineers measure quantity of light in foot-candles. A foot-candle is approximately the amount of light given by a plumber's candle at a distance of one foot. You may be surprised to know how many foot-candles you need for reading small type, for sewing, especially on dark cloth, for close work done in connection with hobbies like cabinet-making, stamp collecting, fly tying.

On page 186 is a table of lighting values for the home. It was prepared by the Illuminating Engineering Society, and they are careful to say that these figures don't necessarily mean perfect lighting, since in some cases even more light may be necessary.

Now of course you can't go running around your house with a foot-candle meter (probably because you haven't got one), so you would like to know exactly how many watts equal one foot-candle and how big a bulb you need in your reading lamp. This is hard to say, first because the number of foot-candles decreases as the square of the distance from the light source. So if the light is up at the ceiling there will be fewer foot-candles on your page than if the light is three feet away. Then an indirect or diffused light gives fewer foot-candles than a direct light; it's better for the eyes, though, so to get the right amount of light you must use bigger bulbs. Third, a good deal of light is absorbed by the surrounding walls, floors, draperies and furnishings; and when a bulb is old and dirty it gives less light than it did when it was new and clean. Colored bulbs give less than white.

On page 188 is another table which you may find useful.

As a general rule, the ceiling ought to reflect between 65% and 80% of the light in the room, the floors between 10% and 20%, and the walls between 35% and 55%.

ILLUMINATION VALUES FOR RESIDENCES.*

These illumination values aim to fit the light to typical home tasks for persons with normal vision, with due consideration to such matters as cost and practical attainability. They do *not* represent the optimum, since under some conditions more light may be necessary, desirable and attainable. The recommended values may be obtained from portable lamps or from special purpose equipment designed for the specific function, or from a combination of local and general lighting.

* *Recommended Practice for Residence Lighting,* prepared by the Committee on Residence Lighting of the Illuminating Engineering Society, reprinted from *Illuminating Engineering,* Vol. 48, No. 8, August, 1953, p. 414.

Specific Visual Tasks	Area To Be Lighted	Footcandles on Task (Current Recommended Practice)
Reading		
Prolonged Periods (smaller type)	14" wide x 12" high	40
Casual Periods (larger type)	14" wide x 12" high	20
Study	14" wide x 12" high	40
Reading Piano Scores		
Advanced (scores with grace notes and fingering notations for complex chords. When score is sub-standard size, and notations are printed on the lines, 100 footcandles or more are needed.)	18" wide x 12" high	40 or more
Intermediate (average scores having notations beside musical notes)	18" wide x 12" high	20
Elementary (simplest scores for beginners)	18" wide x 12" high	10
Writing	14" wide x 12" high	20
Sewing (Hand)		
Dark Fabrics (fine detail, low contrast)	10" x 10"	150 or more
Prolonged Periods (light to medium fabrics)	10" x 10"	80
Occasional (light fabrics)	10" x 10"	40
Occasional (coarse thread, large stitches, high contrast thread to fabric)	10" x 10"	20

Sewing (Machine)		
Dark Fabrics	6″ x 6″	150 or more
Medium Reflectance Fabrics	6″ x 6″	40
Light Fabrics	6″ x 6″	20
Kitchen Duties		
At Sink	40″ wide x 24″ deep	40
At Range	48″ wide x 24″ deep	40
At Work Counters	24″ wide x 20″ deep	40
Laundry		
At Tubs	48″ wide x 20″ deep	40
At Ironing Board	40″ wide x 12″ deep	40
At Ironer	30″ wide x 14″ deep	40
Grooming		
Shaving at Bathroom Mirror	Two planes at right angles to each other 8⅝″ wide x 6″ high plus a 12″ x 12″ plane	40
Make up at Dressing Tables and Dressers	Two planes at right angles to each other 8⅝″ wide x 6″ high	20
Figure Viewing at Full-Length Mirrors		
Critical Inspection	20″ wide x 54″ high	40
Casual Appraisal	20″ wide x 54″ high	20
Handcraft		
At Work Bench	48″ wide x 20″ deep	40
Game Table		
Card Table	30″ x 30″	10
Table Tennis, Recreational	5′ x 9′	20

REFLECTION FACTORS OF TYPICAL PAINT, PAPER, AND WOOD FINISHES FOR INTERIORS *

Color	Per Cent of Light Reflected
White	85
Light	
Cream	75
Gray	75
Yellow	75
Buff	70
Green	65
Blue	55
Medium	
Yellow	65
Buff	63
Gray	55
Green	52
Blue	35
Dark	
Gray	30
Red	13
Brown	10
Blue	8
Green	7
Wood Finish	
Maple	42
Satinwood	34
English Oak	17
Walnut	16
Mahogany	12

* *Recommended Practice of Home Lighting*, Illuminating Engineering Society, December, 1947.

The kind of finish makes a difference, too. A mat finish spreads light evenly, but a gloss finish catches it and reflects it in a few spots, producing glare.

Since it is such a complicated matter to translate foot-candles into watts, engineers have designed some standard lamps and fixtures which will give approximately the required amount of light. You can find out about them from the Lamp Division of the General Electric Company, or from the Illuminating Engineering Society, of 51 Madison Avenue, New York, or from your local power and light company.

On page 190 is a table which will give you an idea of proper sizes of portable lamps and bulbs.

Of course these portable lamps are intended to illuminate the work place itself. They should be used against a background of general illumination.

In the kitchen or laundry, for instance, you need a central fixture to light up the whole room. For a room of 150 to 200 square feet, if you have a central fixture with a globe 12 inches in diameter that diffuses the light, you will need a bulb of 150 watts. You will also need separate lamps at your work centers.

In the living room you should have enough lamps to give general illumination as well as to focus on the individual work places. While you don't want to cut out all contrast and shadow, it is hard on the eyes to read in a circle of light against a dark background, and a room that has only spots of light strains the eyes because they are drawn to the light sources.

This brings us to the quality of the lighting that is best for your eyes. Avoid glare at all costs. Glare is light or brightness in the field of vision that causes discomfort to the eyes and interferes with seeing.

See that there are no unshaded light bulbs. Be careful that shades conceal *all* of the bulb from the eyes. But let the edge of the shade be high enough not to cast its own shadow on your work. (See table p. 190.) Don't have too many shiny surfaces—enam-

DIMENSIONS OF WELL-DESIGNED PORTABLE LUMINAIRES.*

Portable Luminaire Type	Bulb Wattage	Height (Inches) to Bottom of Shade Above Floor	Minimum Shade Diameter Bottom (Inches)	Minimum Shade Diameter Top (Inches)
Large Floor	100-200-300	49	18½	10½
(with circular fluorescent)	32	49	18½	14
Junior Floor	50-100-150	47	16	9½
(with circular fluorescent)	32	47	16	14
Double Swing Arm	50-100-150	47	16	9½
(with circular fluorescent)	32	47	16	14
Bridge	50-100-150	48	13	8½
Table	150	40 (42″ max.) (15–17″ above 25″ high table)	16	8½
Table	150	45 (15″ above 30″ high desk)	16	8½
Table				
(with circular fluorescent)	32	42	16	14
(with 300-watt bowl)	100-200-300	42 (17″ above 25″ high table)	17½	14
Wall	100	Varies with application as noted.	10	6
	150		13	8½
Dresser	100	19 (above dresser)	9½	7
Dressing Table	100	13 (above dressing table)	9½	7

* *Recommended Practice for Residence Lighting*, p. 420.

eled walls, mirrors, and so on—where they will catch direct light. See that shades and globes are not so transparent that they don't diffuse the light properly. See that very sunny windows are softly curtained. Arrange your furniture so that you don't sit facing a light source. Have reflectors or silvered-bowl bulbs in your lamps.

Indirect lighting (light projected upward and reflected off the ceiling) is softest and easiest on the eyes for general illumination but may not be strong enough to light up a work surface.

Never have a reading lamp directly in front of you or directly behind you, but rather at one side.

The Lamp Division of the General Electric Company has worked out "lighting recipes" which you may follow to get the right number of foot-candles for your work.

For instance, to light a desk for studying or drawing, they recommend the following: use a lamp which measures 25 inches to the top of the reflector. The diameter of the reflecting bowl is eight to nine inches. The minimum diameter of the shade bottom is 16 inches and the lower edge of the shade should be 15 inches above the table top. The shade should be light in color but not too transparent to light. Use a 50-100-150 watt three-light bulb or a 150-watt frosted bulb. Use a large pastel blotter to cover the desk top to prevent reflections and avoid contrasts with light-colored papers. Place the center of the lamp base 15 inches to the left of the center of the book or papers and 12 inches in from the front edge of the desk. Place the desk against a light colored wall for best results. This will give you 40 foot-candles of light on your work.

To light a range or sink (in addition to a central kitchen fixture) this recipe is given: use a shielded unit with 25-watt or 40-watt fluorescent tube. Or use a shielded unit with two 60-watt frosted bulbs placed 18 inches apart. The lamps should be mounted parallel to the wall. Attach the fixture to the wall behind the range or sink, with the bottom edge of the shielding no more than 58 inches above the floor. This gives you about 35 or 40 foot-candles.

You may not be able to follow such instructions to the letter but you will get the habit of using *more* light—most people don't use enough—and you will learn to *shield, diffuse* and *direct* the light so as to get the most comfort for your eyes.

Built-in lighting is expensive, but if you can afford it, it is very pleasant, as well as safe and practical. There are no exposed cords to trip over and no dust-catching surfaces to clean.

To have adequate lighting, you need to be sure that you have *adequate wiring.*

Go through your house and be sure you have enough outlets. Extension cords are dangerous because they trip people up, because they get worn and cause short circuits, and because they heat up too fast when they have to carry too much current. You should have a convenience outlet for at least every six feet of wall space.

Unfortunately, most old houses today, and a great many new ones, don't have adequate wiring for the great load of electrical equipment we want to use. In the old days, a fixture in the middle of the room and one or two outlets for lamps were plenty. But now, in addition to increased lighting, we use washing machines, refrigerators, toasters, heaters, radios, television sets, electric blankets, irons, vaccum cleaners—there are more than fifty electrical appliances in general use in American homes, and more are being invented all the time. It's no wonder we blow fuses.

When you go to put a new fuse into the box, you may notice that it is marked "15 amperes." An ampere is a measure of current flowing through a wire, as "gallons per minute" would be a measure of water flowing through a pipe. If your house has a 15-ampere circuit, that means you can use at one time lamps and appliances up to 1500 watts. A watt is a measure of work done, and one ampere of current gives about 100 watts of work.

A toaster uses from 500 to 1000 watts, a coffee maker another 500 to 1000, a small heater 1000, a television set 300, and an iron

1000. You can see that if you have three or four lights on and are using an iron, and then plug in the toaster, you will blow a fuse.

A fuse is a protective device. It is a plug which contains a strip of soft metal. If the wires get too hot, from having too much of a load put on them or from a short circuit, this strip melts and the current is cut off. This keeps the house from catching fire.

There is a temptation, if the fuse has been blown by too heavy a load, to put in a bigger fuse—a twenty-ampere or even a thirty-ampere fuse—or a coin. *Never* do this. It is a trick which will let more current through, so that you can use more appliances at once, but it may also let the wires get too hot and start a fire.

You can easily see that if you plan to install something like a washing machine (375 watts) or an ironer (1650) or a dryer (4500) or a water heater (4000) or an electric range (up to 14,000) you will have to consult an electrician about the wiring. For any big piece of apparatus you will need a separate circuit. But you may even need extra circuits to take care of the portable appliances. Or part of the house may have to be rewired with heavier gauge wire to take care of the extra load. It is important to have large enough wire and also to have enough circuits in a house for two reasons: first, so that you can use as much amperage as you want; and second, because when current passes through a small wire, or over a very long circuit, it loses voltage, which is electrical pressure. This isn't dangerous, but it might be inconvenient if your refrigerator stopped working because you plugged in the toaster or the iron.

So if you're building or rebuilding, consider doing some rewiring. But if your circuit is only 15 amperes and there is nothing you can do about it, keep in mind the safety rule not to have too many appliances working at once, especially not two heating appliances.

Sometimes you will blow a fuse even when you aren't overstepping the bounds. This is because when a heating appliance is first turned on it produces more than its normal wattage, though after it gets red hot the resistance generated cuts down the wattage. You can get a delayed-action fuse which will allow an overload for a few minutes until the appliance heats up, but not long enough to cause trouble.

Be sure you know where the fuse box is and have some extra fuses and a flashlight handy. You might also have some candles and matches within reach, as well as the telephone number of an electrician. And when a fuse is blown don't replace it until you know what made it blow and have remedied the condition. To be sure all is clear, screw a bulb into the fuse socket. If it lights brightly, there is still a short circuit. If it lights only dimly, there is none.

You should know where the controls and switches are on all your electrical equipment. They ought to be easy to get at. But sometimes it seems that engineers stay up nights designing stoves, refrigerators, washing machines with the controls placed so that you practically have to stand on your head to get at them.

Be sure all your appliances are shockproof, and that all your extension cords and appliance cords are in good condition. Use rubber-covered ones where they may get wet, and hang them up straight, not all twisted. Cords are meant to bend, but constant twisting breaks the fine wires inside them. See that there are no exposed wires, and that plugs are securely fastened, and when you pull out a cord take hold of the plug, not the cord itself.

Protect your outlets with caps so that the baby can't poke his wet fingers or an odd bobby pin inside, and see that there are no metal pull chains on lighting fixtures where they can be touched with wet hands.

Have the flush plates of outlets of nonconducting material, and *never* make repairs on wires without first shutting off current.

Check your home for safety in other respects as well. Prevent falls by having lights easy to turn on. The switches should be near room entrances, or if there are light cords, attach luminous pulls to them. Have lights in closets and on stairs, and see that stairs are freshly painted, especially the top and bottom steps. See that there are no loose rugs on slippery floors, no scuffed corners on rugs or linoleum or stair treads. There should be firm railings on stairways and around all open places and low windows, and screens should be firmly fastened. Winders on stairways are especially dangerous. If you have them, put an extra handrail in.

Repair uneven floors, mop up spilled foods, and don't let the family leave toys, rubbers, skates, or other things lying around to be tripped over. Many accidents are caused by disorder.

Prevent fire by seeing that stoves aren't overheated, that walls and floors near them are insulated and that curtains and clothes don't hang near by. Throw out rubbish, rags and papers, and never do dry cleaning in the house with an inflammable solvent. And have a fire extinguisher handy, but be sure it doesn't give off noxious fumes.

Prevent burns by having a firm table top on which to set hot pans, and by making sure that children can't pull hot things down on themselves, or turn on the hot water and get scalded. Have matches out of their reach. Near your stove keep pot holders, salt and soda to put out grease flames, and a tube of butecin picrate or some other burn remedy in case you do get seared. Be sure fireplaces are screened.

See that your equipment is safe. There should be rounded corners, shields on cutting parts, safety locks on wringers, washers, gas stoves and revolving shelves, and heat controls on iron and ironer. There should be a firm step stool.

Know where your first aid kit is and how to use it.

It's a good idea to get a safety check list from your university extension or insurance company, or from the *National Safety Council* in Chicago. Keep it on your bulletin board and make a tour of your house periodically so you'll know it's safe to live in.

Plan your work rooms—and the rest of the house as well—for easy cleaning. The new floor coverings of linoleum, tile and plastic resilient flooring have already been discussed. Of course you know that light colors show every spot, but do you realize that dark ones do the same? In fact, a heel mark or a bit of dust shows up even more on a plain dark blue linoleum than on a light floor. A mottled or marbled pattern is least revealing. Colored tile is better than white for bathroom floors. Walls can be covered with plastic tile, washable paint or paper, or washable plastics or fabrics. Walls can be built of glass brick. Table tops can be of glass or tile or plastic which is scratchproof and stainproof. Furniture can be covered with washable upholstery.

Woodwork and cabinets can be finished in washable enamel in colors that look nice and don't show dirt as white does. Metal window sills are easy to clean. If you like, you can paint your window sills in some darker color instead of white, or cover them with linoleum. They'll be much easier to clean. But if you prefer them white, you can simonize them.

Natural wood finishes are warm looking and require very little cleaning.

Keep mats on those spots on your floors that get the hardest use—in front of the sink and washing machine, at the front door.

Buy dishes, lamps, silver of simple design to eliminate cleaning. Have glass or pottery ash trays instead of metal.

And don't use cleaning materials that will mar a polished surface—harsh cleansers, or coarse steel wool.

Put away the dust-catching bric-a-brac, and store things that aren't in constant use—books, records, music—under cover to keep them from dust.

You may feel that following these suggestions gives your home a bare look. Even the most severely functional room, however, can be beautiful, and the most beautiful ornaments can look dingy if you haven't time to keep them shining.

Clutter in a workroom—or any room—is distracting. Stand at

the doorway of a room and give it the once-over. Does it please you? Do you get the feeling, "This is good," or is it just the same messy old room? If it's the latter, see if you can't give it a lift just by clearing away clutter. We get into the habit of keeping things because some day we might use them. This has been called "woman's besetting sin." It might be better to lack something than to live amid clutter all your life just on the chance of needing it some day.

Certain areas in your home are pressure areas, and you should try to plan your layout so as to cut down on these. First decide what causes the pressure. It may be poor arrangement. But it may be lack of space or poor scheduling.

The bathroom is often a pressure area because of lack of both space and time. There really ought to be a separate one for each person. But few of us can afford such luxury, and we have to struggle along with only one.

First consider the schedule. Getting Father up earlier to shave, and routing the children in and out in turn, will help. Wash the baby in the kitchen to give the others more time. Teen-agers are hard to deal with. They like to spend hours in the bathroom. The girls are bad enough, but when the boys start to shave, it is quite a situation.

Next consider additional equipment. If you can install an extra toilet and wash basin somewhere in the house, it will be a great help. If not, some sort of washing facilities in bedrooms, even the old bowl and pitcher, will relieve congestion in a large family. Electric razors make water unnecessary for shaving. A good mirror with a light over it may be what the teen-ager (or anybody else) finds so attractive in the bathroom. Install one in each bedroom.

Bathrooms with separate compartments are good because several people can use the room at once, but they are very expensive. If you do want to install another bathroom, remember that interior bathrooms are a possibility. You will have to plan for some form of ventilation. But you will have the advantage of not having to open a window, which is always unpleasant in cold weather, and the bathroom will remain warm even when being aired. Besides, you won't need curtains, which are never at their best in a damp, steamy atmosphere.

A bathroom that opens off a bedroom is useful only for the user of that bedroom. Try to plan for both rooms to open off a small central hall.

Pressure may be caused by not giving enough space to work places.

Hobbies, like children, often outgrow their original space. You may have started scribbling at the dinette table, and now, when you are a professional writer, you still find yourself without a settled work place. You scold your family to keep them quiet, when what you need is a study of your own where their noise won't bother you.

Your record collection may be so big that you need a music room. Your books may require a library.

Everybody should be able to work or study at once without waiting for somebody else to get through with the desk. After all, you don't take turns using the bed. You wouldn't rest very well with someone standing beside you saying, "Sleep quicker, I want the pillow."

And although the home must be a rest place as well as a work and play place, many people forget to allow for rest either in their schedules or in their layout.

You should provide for rest places that can be used at any time. First, they should be accessible. This means that there should be a couch in a quiet place, with a cover that won't be hurt by having feet put up on it, where you can relax for five or ten minutes whenever you like. You should not have to make elaborate preparations by taking off and folding a spread, putting aside cushions, fussing with a curtain. Secondly, the rest place should be respected.

Your family should understand that a person who is resting should be helped and not hindered. This means protection from doorbells, telephones and questions. Explain to them the physiological meaning of fatigue, and make bedtime and rest time a pleasant experience, and the children will learn to enjoy rest and not fight it, either in themselves or in others.

There may be pressure because of *inadequate storage facilities.* Storage has already been discussed in Chapter 6. Look at your house now from an over-all point of view.

There are things that must be available daily, such as everyday clothing, linens, dishes, coats, cleaning equipment, tools, books. See if the taking out and putting away of these things is awkward or inconvenient. See if you are making extra steps or creating traffic problems by your methods of storing them.

Other things are used seasonally. Their location is not particularly important. These are things like seasonal clothing, screens, storm windows, garden furniture, sleds, luggage. Maybe you are giving to these things space which could better be used for everyday things.

A third class consists of things used now and then, that need not be right at hand but should be easy to get at: sports equipment, tools, games, folding chairs and tables, musical instruments. Remember that if they are too hard to get at, they won't be used, or if they are, they won't be put away. This gives rise to pressure, too.

Take a bird's-eye view of your closets. See if some of them can be made to take over the functions of a room. A dressing closet or small dressing room takes pressure away from a bedroom, if it is used by two people. One person can sleep, read or dress in the bedroom while the other uses the closet, which may have shelves, drawers and racks, a light, a mirror and a bench.

A closet may be used as a darkroom, thus freeing a whole room from that function.

Or a room can serve as a closet. A little room near the entrance may be fitted out as a closet to hold outdoor clothing, sports equipment, wheeled toys, shopping cart, empty bottles, everything that pertains to going in or out.

In old houses there is sometimes a room off the kitchen that was once a maid's room. It's only big enough for a cot and a chair, but it can be turned into a storeroom for canned goods, cleaning things, tools, out-of-season clothing, or what you will, thus relieving the rest of the house of the burden of storage.

Pressure arises when there is no *adequate provision for overnight guests.* You want your friends to feel free to come to you, you want your children to invite their friends, and it should be possible to have company without disrupting the household too much. This can be done if you have a couch somewhere that is always made up or that can easily be made up, and if you give some thought to the layout. Know in advance where your guest will put his things, where he will dress and sleep. You should not have to fly around at the last minute wondering what to do, and the guest should not have to use a closet in one room, a bureau drawer in another, and a mirror in a third. This makes him feel uncomfortable. Make a place for his things, and even if you have only a folding canvas cot, it should be easily available and setting it up should take only a few minutes. Have a cot drill once in a while if you aren't sure you can do it fast.

When you're entertaining, think through the menu and plan in advance where you will place the dishes, where everybody will sit and, if it's buffet style, what small tables are available for setting plates down.

If it's a children's party, think through the program from beginning to end. Move the furniture in advance. Decide where to put wraps. Arrange the house for games. Write everything down on three by five cards. Everybody will have more fun if you know just what you're doing.

Pressure is caused by the need of some members of the family to take naps or have meals served at odd hours. Try to arrange places for these activities where they will be out of the way and will not interfere with regular routine.

Pressure is often caused by not giving yourself enough time to make plans and decisions. Many of these changes we have been talking about can't be made in a hurry. They require inspiration, and sometimes you just haven't got it. The thing to do in this case is to let your unconscious mind work for you. Stop concentrating on the problem and do something else. Sleep on it. Let your mind play with it. Don't force yourself to decide until you're sure—some of these things are too hard to make over. Ten to one the idea will come to you when you're least expecting it.

Feed your imagination by reading books and magazines. Go to exhibits of new appliances, decorating and lighting schemes, in laboratories and manufacturers' salesrooms. Take the children and encourage them to make notes and take pictures. They will get interested in stoves, dish-washers, furniture, when they learn to look at them from the point of view of the homemaker who wants the most for her money.

To any twelve-year-old, a sofa or a chair is just some lumber his parents happen to have around the house, until he is asked for his opinion of its comfort, looks or practicality, and given a vote in the choice of a new one.

Children like to draw floor plans and make charts. They will get into the habit of looking for new ways to do things, and develop a tolerant attitude toward change.

It is good for children, as well as for adults, to be adaptable, to be able to say, not, "We can't, we've never done it this way," but, "Come on, let's try this new idea."

Chapter 9

Maintenance

KEEPING THE BALL ROLLING

Now you have made some new installations in your home. Let's say you have rearranged your schedule or your budget or your kitchen storage, or all of them. You've rerouted traffic around the edge of the living room instead of right through the middle. You've changed the standing order for dishwashing and for putting away bed linens. You can see that with the changes you've introduced pressure is reduced, tempers are better, things are going more smoothly. And you like it.

How can you keep it that way?

This is the next problem, and it's a serious one. Backsliding is very easy.

We are all creatures of habit, and it's always the path of least resistance to keep on with the old method.

You may say, "Now the way to clear this table is to put everything on the wheeled cart and take the whole load to the kitchen at once." But almost unconsciously you pick up a plate in each hand and start for the kitchen that way, if that is how you have always done it. Or you set the dishes down on the kitchen table instead of on the counter beside the sink, although the standing order says that counter is for dishes to be washed.

Or perhaps your husband puts the vacuum cleaner in the old place instead of in the new cupboard and you tell him, "No, that's not right." Then he gets cross. People don't like to be told they're doing things wrong.

Or you tell young Johnny, "No, the plates don't go there any more," and he says, "Aw, you're always shifting things around."

How can you form new habits and get your family to do the same without too much resistance?

This is a matter of education. Try to think back to something you have learned in the past—something you learned very quickly. When you were little, you quickly found out where your mother kept the cookies. You had no trouble learning to ride a bicycle. You willingly wrote compositions for that nice fifth-grade teacher who praised you and understood so well what you were trying to express. You were glad to learn to bake cake because you knew your mother would say, "Sister is the one who baked this cake. Isn't it delicious?" And, of course, the process of baking the cake was fun too, both the mixing of the flour and milk and eggs into batter, and the companionship with Mother in the kitchen.

All of this means something that teachers know very well: we learn best the things that give pleasure.

Therefore, if you want your family to learn new habits, you must see that they have pleasanter associations with them than with the old ones. There must be visible rewards in the form of fun, approval, credit, beauty, money, or the satisfaction of creative production.

First, the changes have got to be a family project. We can't say this too often. They must feel that the home belongs to all of them, that there is companionship in discussing and improving it, and that what each one wants and does in the home is important not only to himself but to everybody else in the family.

If you have discussed the new installations with them, listened to their suggestions, explained your point of view and the principles of work simplification behind your new plans, they are more likely to feel there is some reason for learning the new habits. If you just tell them what to do and criticize them for not doing it, they will resist.

Let your family see that the change pays off in terms of real savings in money, time or energy, and they will help more willingly.

For instance, you need some shelves put in between the present ones which are too far apart. There may be some expense for materials. Some of your husband's time may be needed. If he thinks it's just some fad which you dreamed up, and which you're going to get tired of in a few weeks, he won't care for the idea. But when you show him how many hundreds of times you will be saved the necessity of lifting off stacks of smaller plates or bowls to get at the larger ones on the bottom, the plan will make sense to his logical masculine mind and he'll be enthusiastic about it.

Consider the personalities of your family and deal with them accordingly. Some of them may be conservatives and always resist change. It takes them longer to learn new ways. Be patient with them. Explain again, calmly. Don't say, "I've told you fifty times already. Why can't you learn?"

Some people feel that the new way is a criticism of them for not doing the job right, and resist change for that reason. If you show your Aunt Jane that not drying the glassware prevents the deposit of lint, she may think you are criticizing her for leaving lint, and insist on drying to show that she doesn't.

Some people lack patience, and if the new habit isn't learned quickly they give up. Some women, for instance, would rather go on sweeping with a broom than teach themselves to run one of the new types of cleaner.

Some people don't like to be taught. They think they are being ordered about. It is best to give such people the feeling that they themselves have formulated the new method. You may almost have to put the words into their mouths to get them to think that *they* thought it up.

Any mother knows how to do this tactfully. Remember how you asked your unwilling four-year-old: "Would you rather take your teddy bear or your panda to bed tonight?" Of course when they're older than four you want to be a little less obvious, but you get the idea.

Then, try to handle the changes as if you were a personnel manager in a plant or store.

First, the workers, including yourself, must want to do the job the new way because they see the sense of it.

Secondly, they must *have* to do it the new way, because the old way is no longer feasible. If the cupboard over the sink now holds cereals and dried fruits instead of dishes, they *can't* put the dishes there but must put them in their new home. Label the new places. Draw the patterns of your utensils on the wall where they are to hang. Cut a paper circle the size of a plate and glue it to the spot on the shelf where the plate belongs.

The thing to do, then, is to work out maintenance procedures at the time the new method is worked out. If the new way is not harder than the old, you stand a good chance of getting to first base.

Habits which are not based on physical rearrangements, but must be motivated by your mind alone, are harder to learn. You may say to yourself, "From now on I will always get gas in the car on the way home. Then I won't have to waste time starting tomorrow, and I won't run out of gas on the road." Or you may solemnly resolve to have enough supplies in the house for the week end, and not have to send somebody out to look for bread and milk in some delicatessen that happens to be open on Sunday. You may have good intentions but fail to carry them out unless you devise some sort of checking procedure.

When you arrange your daily schedule, make check lists.

Keep a running list of jobs to be done from day to day. This is not the same thing as noting down on a calendar each day what is to be done.

For example, you may note on Monday that you have to call the dentist, see the tailor about your suit, buy socks for Johnny, buy lace for Susie's slip, stop at the electric company and ask them to send a man to look at the refrigerator, return library books, take a watch to the jeweler, return empty bottles to the store, send a birthday card to Aunt Agatha. Some of these you will succeed in doing on Monday, some not. They have to be put off for the next day. But by Tuesday you may lose the slip of paper you wrote on Monday, and you may forget some of the errands and go right past the watchmaker's or forget what it was you wanted at the dry goods store. Take a long strip of paper—adding machine tape is good—and write a list of jobs on it and pin it on your bulletin board. Then each day transfer to your memo pad or appointment book the ones you think you will do. As the jobs get done, cross them off the master list.

You may have a separate column for jobs to be done every day or every few days such as getting gas and oil in the car, taking out the ashes, mowing the lawn, watering plants, doing the accounts, getting practicing done, and so on. Don't cross them off, because they are recurrent. Look at this list every day and fit the odd jobs you have to do into your daily schedule.

If this seems like a big chore, remember that you won't have to do it forever. After a short while you'll remember the jobs and do them without reminders. If you can't, it may be that you have some resistance to them. If you always forget to get gas, maybe it means you don't want to for some reason. See if you can think what the reason is. It may be anything from disliking to park at a certain filling station to wishing your husband would pay for the gas out of his money. It may be that you are not the right person to do the job and that it would be better to delegate it to someone else than to force yourself to do it.

Another good trick for getting work done is the "packaged job."

A packaged job is one that is all done up beforehand into a neat routine, so that you can go ahead with it without stopping to plan it. For instance, suppose the family wants to go on a picnic. It's a beautiful day, and nothing would be nicer except that getting ready is such a chore for Mother. But divide the job up into small packages and nobody will be overworked. You can have as many jobs as there are workers. Number them Job 1, Job 2, Job 3, and so on.

Job 1 might be to get the thermos jug and picnic kit assembled, with paper napkins, tablecloth, tea towel, plates, cups and silver, and to fill the jug with milk or iced tea.

Job 2 might be to prepare salad, pickles, vegetables.

Job 3: Prepare the main course—hot dogs, mustard, rolls, potato chips, chicken, or whatever it is to be.

Job 4: Assemble dessert—slice and wrap cake, wash fruit, et cetera.

List these jobs on cards and put them into your reminder file under the heading: Picnics. Keep a few favorite menus with the cards.

You can make a packaged job of packing a suitcase. Have a more or less standard list of the things you generally need when going on a trip—night clothes, slippers, toilet articles, and clothing for the different activities of morning, afternoon and evening—and keep the list in the suitcase. Remember that it may rain. You may go swimming. You may need walking shoes, evening clothes, business papers, tickets, and so on. A check list will help you to lay out the things you need with a minimum of running back and forth, and you will avoid both the error of forgetting some important thing, and that of taking everything but the kitchen sink in order to have all you need.

Setting the table can be a packaged job. Have a list on your bulletin board or on the inside of the closet door. Then the children need not always be asking, "What do you want me to put on the table?" The list is there—plates, knives, forks, spoons, salt, pepper, cups, glasses, bread, butter, napkins—with some items marked B for breakfast, L for lunch, D for dinner.

When there is a company dinner, jobs can be outlined and posted for before- and after-dinner help, and numbered so that the helpers choose their jobs by number and know just what to do.

For instance, Job 1, which will of course be assumed by the head cook, may be to prepare the roast and vegetables, make the gravy, and put food into serving dishes.

Job 2 would be to set the table and fill glasses, and help serve desserts.

Job 3 would be to fill sugar bowl and cream pitcher, prepare bread and butter, arrange salads and fix relishes, and remove dishes.

Then after dinner, Job 1, which the hostess or head cook usually takes, would be to get the dish washing equipment ready, put away leftovers, and, when the dishes are done, put them away.

Job 2 could be the actual washing, while Job 3 is to bring the dishes from the dining room and do the drying, and Job 4 is to scrape and stack the dishes as they are brought in and to dispose of garbage, remove crumbs, run sweeper, and wipe tables.

A little training will soon get your family in the groove. They can take turns at the different jobs so that nobody gets too bored by doing the same thing all the time, and at the same time everybody gets into the habit of doing all these necessary things.

Other packaged jobs that we are used to doing are fire drills, air raid drills, first aid, life saving. Here of course we are practicing the formation of habits which we hope will never be needed, but which would be very important if they were.

Marketing can be turned into a packaged job. When you make out your shopping list, group the things you need according to where they are to be found in the store—fresh fruits and vegetables together, meats together, soaps and cleaners together, canned goods, dairy foods, cereals together. You usually know your stores well enough to do that. Then you can make a continuous trip through the store instead of tracking back and forth. Also, if you have one or more helpers you can tear the list into parts, giving one part to each helper, and letting them go off and get things from the shelves independently.

Arrange your check list of supplies in the same way. Make it on a large sheet of cardboard, so that it will last a long time. Group meats together; breads, cookies and cake; canned vegetables, fruits and juices; canned soups, meats, fish; and so on down the list. Go through your supply closet and list everything you use. When you make out your shopping list you can quickly run your eye down the columns and see what you need. If you have definite storage places in your cupboards for each kind of supply, you can see at a glance which are missing or running low. And, of course, as soon as any item is used up you should make a note of it on your shopping list.

Another good thing is to have a list of the supplies kept in the refrigerator or somewhere near by—even on the inside of the door—and items scratched off as they are used. Then you always know what the available supplies are, and you plan to use up everything. In this way nothing gets pushed to the back and forgotten.

You can make your lists according to two plans. One is to make menus for three or four days or a week in advance and buy everything you will need for the meals you have planned. Another way is to buy a variety of the things you need, plus whatever you see in the store that seems good, and make up your meals each day from the supplies on hand. Probably most housewives use a combination of both methods. Making the menus first keeps you from going too wild in your buying, as you might otherwise be tempted to buy out the store. The second method is good, as it allows you to take advantage of good buys and the meats and vegetables that look freshest. It also leaves you free to plan your meals to suit your moods, the weather, and the number of people for whom you are cooking.

Thus, by maintaining a supply of food on hand that will not spoil, you can assemble quick meals if surprise company drops in. Of course if you have a freezer you need never be at a loss. Some people go even further than simply having the raw materials in the house. They plan menus for groups of four, six, even eight, combine the frozen supplies for a whole meal in one large package, and then, when the freezer lid is opened, there it is ready to take out without stopping to plan or searching for separate items.

Canned and preserved fruits and vegetables could be arranged in the same way. A supply of packaged mixes makes hot breads and fresh cakes easy to fix. And when you're baking a cake, bake two and put one in the freezer and use it within the next few weeks.

Of course something ought to be said about quantity buying. If you have the storage space, you can save money by buying cases of canned goods, soap, bottled drinks, paper supplies. Some foods are improved by aging—cheeses, honey, wine. But others spoil unless the temperature and humidity are right. Dried fruit, cereals, oranges, potatoes, onions, flour will spoil in a warm or damp place. So you have to be careful not to buy too much.

Larger containers, of course, are more economical than small ones. But there is a danger, if you open a large can of peaches, that it won't be finished, that your family won't want peaches again right away, and that the remainder may stand around until it spoils. You may get in the habit of serving the same foods so often that your family gets tired of them. You don't want to be greeted by a chorus of "What! Peaches again!" Or, on the other hand, you may buy a large amount of some food and then put it aside until its quality has passed the peak.

To avoid these mistakes, date your supplies when you store them, and use them in order of purchase. It is well to use canned foods within a year after they have been processed, and some foods, having a high acid content which may react on the cans, should be used even sooner. When you are buying quantities of food, figure as you would do for canning, preserving or freezing. For example, if you are canning green beans, you will decide how often your family would like to have them. If they would like them once a week, then about fifty containers—quarts or pints, depending on the size of the family—will be enough. There may be some weeks when you will use more than one, but on the other hand part of the year there will be fresh garden supplies which you will want to use.

Be sure you don't get so much of an out-of-season food like strawberries or asparagus canned or frozen that your family doesn't appreciate the fresh ones when they appear in the spring.

Storage space is important for any supplies, but it is really vital for frozen foods, so be sure you don't pack more than your freezer will hold. Each cubic foot will hold about twenty-five pounds in cylindrical or odd-shaped packages, or about forty pounds in brick-shaped packages. And it's a good idea to keep a check list of the contents of your freezer and cross off the packages as you use them so you don't plan on something you haven't got.

Your cleaning supply closet can have a check list too, to let you know when you are low on soaps, polishes, waxes and cleansers.

And have a check list of linens as part of your household notebook. It is very convenient to know exactly how many sheets you have, how many towels, pillow cases and wash cloths, and in what condition. Some wear out faster than others, and then you buy more, and mend the old ones, and the first thing you know, it's a gamble when you take a sheet from the closet whether it will have a seam down the middle or whether it will be one you bought last week.

If you like you can keep a record of size, brand, purchase date and price of each type of linen. Then you can compare the amount of wear you get from different brands. If you don't want to go to all this trouble, simply make an inventory of your linen, and when a sheet or pillow case wears out, deduct it from the total. A good time to make such an inventory is around the date of the white sales in the stores.

An excellent way to classify linen is to put all the information you need on the linen itself. Mark the bottom hem of each sheet with the size, date of purchase, and your name. Then you can quickly tell in which pile to stack it, you have an idea from its age whether to be on the lookout for tears, and you have some insurance against loss in the laundry. You can mark those pieces that are reserved for special beds, such as guest beds, children's beds or camp with different colored tape or thread, and when a piece is worn out mark it by sewing diagonally across it with a colored thread to show that it can now be used for cleaning rags.

It is convenient and time-saving to mark and date other things besides linen. Clothing can be marked with ink or with name tapes to help children identify their mittens, boots, coats and hats at school. Put a red cross stitch or some other specific mark at the collar of shirts or on the top edge of socks to show your husband that they are mended and should be worn for jobs around the house and not to the office. Put an X on children's caps and polo shirts and boxer pants to show which is the front.

All the above suggestions are made to help you to maintain the new ways of doing work which you have installed.

Now suppose that in spite of all your efforts and good intentions, some of your new methods just don't work. You've rearranged Johnny's room and he still doesn't keep it in order. You've made yourself a schedule and you still can't manage time to rest in the afternoon. How can you get better results?

Well, first consider what an engineer would do if the results he expected in the factory were not forthcoming. Would he just give it up as a bad job and say that this efficiency stuff is a lot of nonsense anyhow? No. He would check up on things.

If he found he wasn't getting the quota of work he expected, he might ask whether the standards he had set up were too high to be met by the workers. He would ask whether the workers understood and cared about the standards that were expected. He would ask whether the right people were actually at work on the job, and whether they were really working according to the methods he had set up, and if so, whether those methods were really practical. He would ask whether the equipment, tools and supplies he had set up as necessary for the job were really being used.

You should do the same sort of thing. Don't get discouraged, and say this efficiency business is more trouble than it's worth. Constitute yourself and your family a Committee of Investigation and see where the plans went wrong. It's time for another conference.

Have you really agreed on your standards? Do you know what they are? Are they too high? Some people can decide it isn't necessary to strip the beds every day, and yet go right on doing it because way down inside themselves they are still clinging to the old standard and haven't agreed to the new one at all. Naturally the bed-making will take more time than is allowed in the schedule and this and other things will cut into the time set down for a rest period.

Find out whether you are a perfectionist. Sometimes a perfectionist in the family brings too much pressure to bear on those who are not so rigid in their requirements. You may have fixed up Johnny's room beautifully, you may have arranged a lovely study for your husband, but if they feel you've got your eye on them and are silently criticizing them for not keeping things picked up, they may shy away from the task and just not do it at all.

On the other hand, if you have changed standards in some respect, see if you have really arranged for the new standard to be carried out. For instance, if you have decided that when there is no company the family will eat in the kitchen instead of in the dining room, be sure you aren't moving your dining room procedure into the kitchen. You're doing this to save work, and therefore you won't use the good tablecloth and china and silver serving dishes. You'll use plastic mats and sturdy everyday pottery. You'll either serve from the stove, or use cooking utensils that can double as serving dishes. Of course you don't want to get way down to Tobacco Road standards and stick the old black frying pan in the middle of the table, but you will manage so that everything is more informal, while still remaining neat and attractive.

In other words, don't use sterling silver standards where stainless steel would be more appropriate. This is a problem that young married people often have to deal with quite firmly.

They are lucky enough to get a lovely set of silver for a wedding present. Silver is beautiful and gracious and something you want to keep for your children and all that, but it requires lots of loving care. If you have it, you want to use it. Then you must have china to go with it. You wouldn't use ordinary crockery with your elaborate silver. Then you need table linen. And then of course you wouldn't put fine linen, china and silver on any old pine table. You'd want nice furniture. And then there would have to be rugs and curtains to match. So before you knew it you would have your whole house furnished according to a sterling silver standard, requiring quantities of time and elbow grease to keep in order, when what you really should have started with was a set of stainless steel. It never needs polishing, it doesn't scratch, you can dump it into the dishpan, it goes with all informal furnishings, and it sets a standard that leaves you free to paint, wash diapers, hold a job, or fill whatever other role life has cast you for.

The homemaker who holds a job has to be especially careful not to cling too hard to a set of standards that dates back to the time when the lady of the house was always at home, and moreover had servants to help her.

If you feel satisfied with your standards, but still think things aren't working out quite right, examine your schedules. It may be that you have crowded too much into one day and not enough into another. You need different work patterns for different days. The day that the laundry must be done, the day that the cleaning woman comes, or week ends when the entire family are at home require schedules lighter in some respects because they are heavier in others. Or it may be that your schedule looks very nice on paper, but actually does not allow for a number of things that you are doing. If the schedule says that you are to wash the dishes, make the beds, make a shopping list, go to market, come home and get lunch, and you squeeze in half an hour's telephoning, mop the kitchen floor, rinse out a few clothes and write a letter, you can't expect the schedule to work. See that you allow time for *all* the things you need to do, or firmly put off some of them so as not to get too far behind.

Make a check on time every so often in the course of your work. Cast your eye on the clock and see if you're keeping up to running time, at least until you get used to the schedule.

If you find the family always breaking into your schedule, set up a notification rule. This gives you a chance to get ready for interruptions. You might make it a rule that a child must give a day's notice before bringing a guest to a meal. You won't stick to it rigidly, because lots of times when the children are playing and Johnny asks whether Stevie can stay to supper you want to say yes at once, so Johnny knows his friends are welcome. But if it happens to be a busy time you can fall back on the rule and Johnny will respect it. You might ask your husband to give you at least a few hours' notice before bringing a guest. Guests themselves might be gently persuaded to telephone in advance of arrival. Or you may wish to have it known that you have open house every Sunday afternoon, or the last Sunday of the month, when all are welcome.

Check your schedule of recurring tasks—the daily, weekly, monthly, seasonal or annual jobs. Don't forget to look at your calendar every day. It's all very well to make a note of things to be done, but you have to turn the pages of the calendar pad to be reminded of them, and if you have a reminder file you have to consult it. Have a regular time, say Saturday morning, for the family to get together to list jobs to be done. Then they can volunteer to do certain jobs and schedule the time for them.

When customs are established they become easy. Saturday night used to be bath night in many households. Everybody took a bath because it was expected (and also because he was pretty dirty by then and it seemed necessary).

Suppose repairs don't get done around your house. You can make Tuesday night "repair night." All the little jobs of mending chair rungs, fixing lamp sockets, planing doors, can be set aside until that time (unless they are very urgent and cannot possibly be postponed—a plumbing leak, for instance). In one household the repair procedure is to have everyone who sees a job needing to be done list it at once. The person who sees the need gets the credit, but is not necessarily penalized by being made to do the job. Thus there is real motivation. There is a record book attached to the bulletin board, and once a week the jobs are discussed and handed out to those best qualified to do them. The discussion gives a good opportunity to ask questions. Why did this happen? Could it have been prevented? What should we do to keep it from happening again?

This sort of questioning leads to long-term planning and makes maintenance a family project.

If work isn't done right, check on your standing orders. See if they are written so clearly as to be easily understood, and if they give reasons for jobs. See if instruction sheets are kept in their proper places—in the file, or with the tool or apparatus they apply to. Then see if the worker has read the instructions. Some people don't like to read. Others find it hard to assimilate written instructions and put them into practice.

Some people need to be reminded but don't like to be told. This applies particularly to children. The sound of your voice urging them to tidy their room or take the dog for a walk seems to them like nagging. Try leaving a little note. A silent reminder is more subtle. They don't have to answer it politely if they don't want to.

Check on the work methods and how they are being maintained. See if you are really using the principles of motion economy. Here is a check list worked out by the American Heart Association. It was meant to be used in connection with the work simplification kitchen which they designed. You may find it useful in your home. Some parts of it may not apply in your case, and on the other hand you may want to add many questions that don't appear in it.

The Motion Study Check List *

A. The Job
1. Why is it necessary that this job be done at all?
2. What is the purpose to be accomplished?
3. Where can it best be done; in this kitchen or elsewhere?
4. Who is best fitted to do this job?
5. When is the best time to do it?
6. How can this job be simplified?
7. Can the *Get ready* or *Clean up* be reduced:
   By combining two or more jobs, tools, materials?
   By larger size batches?
   By changing sequence of jobs?
   By planning *Clean up* to save *Get ready* of next job?

B. The Layout
1. Are work centers in proper sequence to avoid back tracking?
2. Are work centers close together to save steps without crowding?
3. Can incoming supplies be stored effectively without unnecessary handling for the kitchen operation?

* Reprinted from *Heart of the Home*, American Heart Association, New York, N.Y., p. 9.

4. Are floors smooth surface, free of irregularities, projections, steps or door sills?
5. Is there sufficient aisle space to permit use of wheeled carts or mobile work tables?

C. The Work Place

1. Is each work center arranged so that tools, materials and utensils are within the normal work area?
2. Is the work height arranged to reduce fatigue by alternately sitting and standing?
3. Is work level for the hands at comfortable elbow height?
4. Must tools, materials or utensils be raised and lowered unnecessarily during use?
5. Are holding devices provided to relieve hands, thereby reducing fatigue and promoting safety?
6. Are fixed work stations provided for equipment like can openers, mounted at proper working height?
7. Are waste materials disposed by gravity into foot-pedal-operated containers?
8. Are work surfaces smooth, level, and free of crevices for ease in cleaning?
9. Is there a place for all necessary things, and all unnecessary things eliminated?

D. Tools and Equipment

1. Are tools properly designed for safe effortless operation, ease of cleaning and maintenance?
2. Are tools pre-positioned for quick grasp and easy disposal?
3. Are shelves at comfortable height to avoid stooping or climbing, and arranged so that most frequently used items are close at hand?
4. Can utensils be selected without undue search and handling?
5. Can drawers or doors be opened with minimum effort?

6. Are chairs provided with posture seats, adequate back and foot rests?
7. For constant standing jobs, are there suitable back rests or support?

E. Materials and Supplies
1. Are they conveniently stored near point of use?
2. Can gravity feed hoppers be used for materials like flour, sugar, etc?
3. Can containers be easily cleaned, round inside corners, etc.?

F. Work Methods
1. Does the worker use the simplest, shortest motion path?
2. Are both hands usefully occupied at the same time?
3. Does worker use circular, rhythmic motions at a smooth, steady work pace?
4. Are periodic rest periods arranged or frequent change of occupation to reduce monotony and overcome fatigue?

G. Working Conditions
1. Is there sufficient illumination, evenly distributed, properly color balanced, without glare or sharp contrast?
2. Are walls, floors, counters and curtains blended into a cheerful, harmonious color scheme?
3. Is worker supplied with sufficient fresh air, free of dust, fumes, odors?
4. Are temperature, humidity and air circulation within comfortable limits?
5. Are surroundings pleasant, quiet (sound conditioned), properly related to adjoining living areas, and view of outdoors (picture window)?

You may think you have followed all the rules, and yet there may be a feeling of tension or pressure in your home. If this is so, check on possible causes. Tension does no harm if it occurs once in a while as a result of some emergency or sudden shift in plans, but as a general rule it is bad for most of us. Different people react with tension to many things. Here are some of them.

1. *Lack of time for the job.* A worker who hates to feel rushed should be encouraged to find his own pace and to examine his schedule.

2. *Fear of inadequacy.* If the worker really isn't able to do the work, he should be relieved of it or helped. If he is capable, he should be encouraged and taught.

3. *Worry.* People who are upset and worried don't work well, whether the anxiety is about the job they are doing or about some other matter. If you can't eliminate it, at least see that the job isn't blamed for off-the-job happenings.

4. *Distaste for the job* because of noise, dust, grease, or for any other reason. If you can find the physical cause of the dislike and remove it, well and good. If this is impossible because of the nature of the work, perhaps somebody who doesn't find it distasteful can take over the job. Some people don't mind noise, others love to muck around in oil and grease, still others enjoy working with soap suds. Of course if the worker can discipline himself to do the work, so much the better, but if not, different people may alternate on the job so that all share distasteful as well as attractive jobs.

5. *Dislike of surroundings, equipment and tools, or fear of using certain tools.* First find out the reasons. Improve the surroundings whenever possible, using the suggestions of the unhappy worker if you can. Be sure the use of the equipment is thoroughly understood. If this is impossible, you may have to transfer the worker from the job. Some people never learn to squeeze oranges with an electric mixer or run an ironer, but continue to have accidents, and it's better not to force them.

6. *Dislike of method.* Some people just won't learn a new method. An older worker, a woman who has kept house for many years, will only be disturbed if you insist. So if you've tried all

sorts of explanations and suggestions, you'll probably have to let her do it her own way.

7. *Unsatisfied cravings for appreciation.* You may not realize that your helpers, or you yourself, are not getting proper thanks for the work that is being done. Everyone needs a reward. But often in the rush of our daily life we assume that "if I don't complain, you are doing well." This satisfies no one. Of course an undue craving for appreciation should be looked into, but don't forget that even the Cat Who Walked by Himself wanted some words of praise.

8. *Uncertainty as to what is wanted.* This goes back to the standing order, which should be clear and definite.

9. *Interfering rhythm.* This is a subtle cause of tension, as the worker himself may not recognize it. Some people, especially musical ones, are very much annoyed by interrupting noises and rhythms.

10. *Conscious or unconscious tension in general.* This, of course, affects the worker's entire life, of which housework is only a small part. If you feel that there is general tension, which is not remedied by any superficial treatment, of course it must be dealt with by methods beyond the province of this book.

11. *Social demands of the job.* Check again to see whether the worker is lonesome and needs group activity, or whether for some reason she dislikes group activity and wants to be alone—whether she has any prejudices (race, sex, creed, age, social group) that prevent happy group work. Find out whether the people with whom she has to work are distasteful to her for any other reasons, and whether she herself is an asset to the group. Often it seems so sensible to enlist the help of an aunt or a grandmother or a maid or a friend, until you find that people don't get along well together. It is up to you to help the different members of your household work together as a team, and you can often work wonders by understanding what each individual wants and needs.

Finally, give your whole house a general inspection. Plan a

regular time for this, and make the grand tour. Take your husband and children along, if possible. See if doors and windows open smoothly, if floors are even, if drawers slide well. Check on your equipment and tools. Are they in good condition, and are you actually using them and storing them as you planned? If you aren't, there must be a reason. Either the plan wasn't suitable or a compromise was necessary, or things have been allowed to slip.

See if all safety precautions have been met. Keep an eagle eye open for repairs on this tour of inspection, and make a note to have them taken care of, either by a member of the family or by an outside "fixer."

When you've done all these things, or as many of them as you feel you need to do, you'll be surprised by a beautiful reward. Your home will function smoothly. It may not be spotless, but in the main it will be a tidy home, without clutter, with no unfinished jobs strewn about where they don't belong, and with that "at-ease" feeling that makes friends and family want to be there.

Chapter 10

Facing the Future

Maintenance means keeping things stable. It means setting standards and sticking to them.

But this alone isn't enough. The person who clings too closely to his standards becomes rigid. So, along with the methods you have set up for maintaining your standards, you must keep the ability to change when it becomes necessary.

This is being flexible.

Change must come to all of us. Some changes we choose for ourselves, as you did when you installed new work methods in your home. Other changes come whether we will or no, and it is up to us to be ready for them. They may be such slight changes as the children's desire to skip their bath and stay up to see a program on television, or your sudden decision not to cook today but to go out for dinner. Sometimes it's fun to break rules, or to make plans on the spur of the moment. Being ready for changes like these involves nothing more than an open mind.

On the other hand, changes can be of a more serious nature. Financial difficulties, illness, fire, flood, earthquakes, death, war—these are changes that we would all shrink from facing if we could. And sometimes fear of them makes us behave like ostriches. We accept the fact that they can happen to others, but we resist the possibility of their happening to us. So we fail to prepare for them, only to find that we must endure an emotional shock as well as unexpected demands on our money, time and energy. It is as if we said to ourselves, "Be unprepared. What isn't planned for probably won't happen."

The best way to meet these unforeseen changes is by planning. It would be very nice to sit back and say, "The Lord will provide." But this attitude would be more suitable for babies and the birds of the air. Actually the Lord does provide. He provides us with brains, and it is up to us to use them.

How can we plan for change? The first thing to do is to ask ourselves what changes are inevitable. Certain changes come to every family. Death must be faced. Illness appears. Taxes may go up. The cost of living rises.

We can cushion the material shock of these changes by means of different kinds of insurance and savings. It's worrisome and annoying to spend money on insurance or keep funds in a savings account when there are so many immediate needs that have to be met. But it's much more depressing to face the changes unprepared. Only a family that has had that experience can really know what it means.

The important thing about insurance is that you have to be willing to lose. When you buy life insurance and accident insurance you certainly don't want to cash in on them. So you have to consider that you are not just wasting money on premiums, or losing its value by keeping it in the bank, but buying peace of mind. Then, if the event doesn't happen, hooray! You can celebrate. Overcaution, skimping the present to provide for a carefree future, is of course foolish. But it's a great asset to know where you stand.

But material preparation isn't all. How can we be emotionally ready for changes? By accepting the fact that they may come, and by taking some thought as to how we had better behave when they do.

We know that when a great disaster like a flood or an earthquake or a war strikes, we behave in general with great courage. We all put our shoulders to the wheel. We obey orders, we make shift with what we have, we give up things we value, from pots and pans to our own blood, even our own children. We take pride in our ability to work together for a common cause.

Families should be able to work together in a sudden emergency or even in case of changes that aren't necessarily emergencies.

Some changes give us plenty of warning—we can see them coming.

Neighborhoods change, but not overnight. We can decide whether we want to go on living in them and adapting ourselves to new ways or whether we want to move, which involves other changes.

Children grow up. We have to change our ways of dealing with them, according to their ages. We have to say to ourselves, gently but firmly, "When this child was three or four, I led him across the street by the hand. But now he's bigger, he must learn to go alone some of the time."

If the event we're anticipating is a pleasant one, planning for it is easy. Everybody loves a wedding or a new baby.

But if the event is unpleasant, it is a different matter. Sometimes a son or daughter marries someone the family doesn't like. How would you behave if you were suddenly faced with this situation? You would have to school yourself to get to know the new member of the family and *learn* to like him or her.

Sometimes an aunt or grandmother or a parentless child comes into a home that is already somewhat crowded. How would you act if it were your home? Would you show resentment that you were unable to hide or would you teach your family to welcome the newcomer? We all know how necessary it is to be wanted, not rejected. The wanted person, child or adult, is a happy one and so is the family that welcomes him, not just as a newcomer but as a very special person—the one who tells good stories, or who makes delicious cakes, or who knows such good games or is always so much fun.

Changes in budget mean new problems. Of course everybody will say it's easy to expand a budget. But sometimes it's difficult to expand reasonably. A small increase in income may warrant buying some new furniture. But then there may be a temptation to go on from there to entertaining more, to traveling more, to moving to a more expensive neighborhood, until the family is in deeper waters than they bargained for.

Contracting a budget is a stiff job. What would you do if your husband suddenly lost his job and had to take another one at a lower salary? Would you feel angry and sorry for yourself and put upon? Or could your family make the problem into a challenge, cut where it hurts least, even have a little fun with the project? If they can, it will be a wonderful exercise in adaptability, but it won't be easy, for it means they must neither make a virtue of poverty nor try to keep on living as they did before. It means they must cling to the most important of their standards, and let the more superficial ones go.

You have to be more or less prepared for changes in yourself. What would you do if you suddenly found yourself with a good deal less energy than usual? Would you push yourself relentlessly ahead until you dropped? Would you collapse on the sofa and let yourself be pampered? Or would you take stock of what you could do and make the best of the situation while you tried to build yourself up again?

Some of us get arthritis, or high blood pressure, or other things unpleasant to contemplate. *All* of us get older. We have to adapt ourselves to our own new conditions and to changes in the world around us.

Here is where your motionmindedness pays off. When you're young and full of pep you can use it to get more work done, to go from homemaking to a paid job outside the home. When your energy budget is decreased you can carry your job techniques back to your home, and find new interests there. If the time comes when you and your husband want to retire and take life easy, you may both get a lot of fun out of making housework into a team job.

Changes in your time budget need flexibility, too. Just as you may decide to spend a little more money than you can afford on a very special birthday present, sometimes you have to give more time than you would like to some project. Your P.T.A. chairman may draft you to telephone all the parents in your child's class for a special meeting. Maybe you haven't got the hour to spare, but you take it.

Or the baby gets sick, just when you planned to catch up on sleep.

Or your best friend has a quarrel with her husband. She has to have somebody to talk to. You were going shopping, but you put it off and stay home and hold her hand till she feels better.

Flexibility, then, means tolerance. It means freedom from hidebound tradition. It means you can use your imagination and your creative ability to get new ideas to meet changing situations.

Suppose you're accustomed to marketing twice a week. But now you can't carry such a heavy load, or the elevator breaks down and you can't use your shopping cart, or your schedule is changed so that you go downtown each day, and come home on the bus in your good clothes. You can buy a few things at a time each time you go past the store, and keep up your inventory that way.

Suppose you're used to cleaning your whole house every Friday. But suddenly you haven't time, or the work gets too hard. You can clean one room each day and never have to do a complete housecleaning.

Would you be embarrassed if a neighbor came in and found your house topsy-turvy, dishes in the sink, beds unmade, and you in bathrobe and slippers at eleven in the morning? If you're meeting a deadline and haven't a second to spare you won't worry about it.

Flexibility means willingness to face the future, and this is one of the great contributions the homemaker can make. Nobody really knows what the future will bring, but you as the mother of your family can give your husband and children the conviction that whatever happens, you can face it together. Nothing gives a family greater courage and assurance than to know that someone in it has this conviction. Feelings of uncertainty in the world today make children jittery, make the man of the family tense and anxious. Somebody has to feel sure that the family will go on, that life will go on, that there may be troubles but that we're working toward a goal, not toward empty failure. And the best person to have it and to radiate it is you.

One thing we know—there will always be work for our hands to do, and this is good. If we can love our work, and love the family and friends for whom we work, we may in time learn to love the larger family of people of which we are all a part.

Change is inevitable. It has been said, the only thing we are sure of is change. We must not fear it. We can't go back; there is only one way to go and that is ahead. We may seem to have lost a great deal, but the essential things remain. The Bible tells us what they are.

"And now remaineth three things, faith, hope, love. And the greatest of these is love."

Picture Credits

Grateful acknowledgment is made for permission to use, as the basis for drawings, photographs from the following publications:

Ella M. Cushman, *Centers for Your Work and Leisure,* Cornell Extension Bulletin No. 811, New York State College of Home Economics, Ithaca, N.Y. Drawing on page 148.

Heart of the Home, Pictorial Supplement, American Heart Association, New York, N.Y. Drawings on pages 134, 135, 154 and endpapers.

Mary Koll Heiner and Helen E. McCullough, *Kitchen Cupboards that Simplify Storage,* Cornell Extension Bulletin No. 703, New York State College of Home Economics, Ithaca, N.Y. Drawings on pages 133, 136, and 139. Diagrams on pages 118 and 137.

Household Storage Units, Circular C5.1, Small Homes Council, University of Illinois, Urbana, Ill., based on material by Helen E. McCullough, Department of Home Economics. Drawings on pages 141 and 149.

Posture in Housework, Extension Service, U. S. Department of Agriculture, Washington, D.C. Drawings on pages 102, 103, 106, 107, 112, and 113.

Rx for the Disabled Housewife, Institute of Physical Medicine and Rehabilitation, New York University–Bellevue Medical Center, New York, N.Y. Drawing on page 128.

Floor plans on pages 168 and 169 are from *Easier Homemaking,* Station Bulletin No. 529, Agricultural Experiment Station, Purdue University, Lafayette, Ind.

Floor plans on pages 173, 174 and 175 are from *Your Farmhouse—Planning the Kitchen and Workroom,* U. S. Department of Agriculture Home and Garden Bulletin No. 12, Bureau of Human Nutrition and Home Economics, Washington, D.C.

Bibliography

BOOKS

Abel, Dorothy Lois. *Making Housekeeping Easy.* New York: F. S. Crofts Company, 1948.

Agan, Tessie. *The House, Its Plan and Use.* Philadelphia: J. B. Lippincott Company, 1948.

Barnes, Ralph M. *Motion and Time Study.* New York: John Wiley & Sons, Inc., 1949.

Cushman, Ella Mary. *Management in Homes.* New York: Macmillan Company, 1945.

Donaldson, Elvin F. *Personal Finance.* New York: Ronald Press Company, 1948.

Gilbreth, Lillian M. *The Home Maker and Her Job.* New York: D. Appleton–Century Company, 1938.

Gillies, Mary Davis. *How to Keep House.* New York: Harper & Brothers, 1949.

Gross, I. H. and Crandall, E. W. *Home Management in Theory and Practice.* New York: F. S. Crofts Company, 1947.

Nickell, Paulena and Dorsey, Jean Muir. *Management in Family Living.* New York: John Wiley & Sons, Inc., 1950.

Radell, Neva Henrietta. *Financial Planning for the Individual and Family.* New York: F. S. Crofts Company, 1948.

Sleeper, Catherine and Harold R. *The House for You to Build, Buy or Rent.* New York: John Wiley & Sons, Inc., 1948.

Tuomey, Douglas. *Home Maintenance Handbook.* New York: Funk and Wagnalls Company, 1948.

Wright, Mary and Russell. *Guide to Easier Living.* New York: Simon and Schuster, Inc., 1950.

PAMPHLETS

Contemporary Houses Developed from Room Units, Small Homes Council, University of Illinois, Urbana, Illinois.

Contemporary Lighting in Modern and Transitional Interiors,

Illuminating Engineering Society, 51 Madison Avenue, New York 10, N.Y.

Easier Homemaking, Bulletin 529, Agricultural Experiment Station, Purdue University, Lafayette, Indiana.

Handbook of Kitchen Design, Small Homes Council, University of Illinois, Urbana, Illinois.

Handbook of Residential Wiring Design, Industry Committee of Interior Wiring Design, 420 Lexington Avenue, New York, N.Y.

Heart of the Home, New York Heart Association, 2 East 103 Street, New York, N.Y.

Household Storage Units, Circular C5.1, Small Homes Council, University of Illinois, Urbana, Illinois.

Kitchen Cupboards that Simplify Storage, by Mary Koll Heiner and Helen E. McCullough. Cornell Extension Bulletin 703, New York State College of Home Economics, Ithaca, N.Y., 1951.

Light Conditioning Recipes for the Home, Lamp Department, General Electric Company, Nela Park, Cleveland, Ohio.

Posture in Housework, Extension Service, U. S. Department of Agriculture, Washington, D.C.

Recommended Practice of Home Lighting, Illuminating Engineering Society, 51 Madison Avenue, New York, N.Y.

ORGANIZATIONS AND OTHER SOURCES OF MATERIAL

American Heart Association, 1775 Broadway, New York 19, N.Y.

Cornell University Agricultural Experiment Station, Ithaca, N.Y.

Government Printing Office, Washington, D.C.

Illuminating Engineering Society, 51 Madison Avenue, New York, N.Y.

Institute of Physical Medicine and Rehabilitation, 400 East 34 Street, New York 16, N.Y.

Lamp Department, General Electric Company, Nela Park, Cleveland, Ohio.

National Adequate Wiring Bureau, 155 East 44 Street, New York 17, N.Y.

National Safety Council, Inc., Chicago, Illinois.

Purdue University Agricultural Experiment Station, Lafayette, Indiana.

Small Homes Council, University of Illinois, Urbana, Illinois.

United States Department of Agriculture, Washington, D.C.

Index